60p

**Empress
Matilda**

By the same author

The King and Becket
George III At Home

Empress Matilda

Uncrowned Queen of England

NESTA PAIN

Weidenfeld and Nicolson · London

Printed in Great Britain by
Butler & Tanner Ltd,
Frome and London

Contents

Illustrations

Acknowledgements

The author and publishers are grateful for permission to reproduce illustrations:

Matilda's seal from the Mansell Collection; coronation of Emperor Henry from a manuscript at Corpus Christi College, Cambridge, photograph Bavaria Verlag; plaque of Geoffrey of Anjou from Musée du Mans; Channel crossing from the Bayeux tapestry, photograph Michael Holford; Angers, photograph Jean Roubier; dinner scene from Bayeux tapestry, photograph Michael Holford; siege from Bayeux tapestry, photograph Michael Holford; Falaise, photograph Jean Roubier; weaving from Eadivine's Psalter, Trinity College, Cambridge; siege of Jerusalem from Pierpont Morgan Library, photograph Snark International; initial from Kelso Charter by kind permission of the Duke of Roxburghe, photograph National Library of Scotland; Devizes Castle from *Devizes Castle, Its History and Romance* compiled by E. Herbert Stone, photograph Wiltshire Archaeological Society; Bristol Castle from *The History and Antiquities of the City of Bristol* by William Barrett, 1789; Oxford Castle from *The Antiquities of England and Wales*, vol. III, by Francis Grose, 1775; reliquary in the Musée des Antiquités, Rouen, photograph by Ellébé; Matilda's representation, photograph Wiltshire Archaeological Society.

Picture research by Philippa Lewis

The translation on page 161 of Stephen's Charter November 1153 is from *English Historical Documents*, volume II, edited by David Douglas (Eyre & Spottiswoode).

1 Childhood and Marriage

If the Empress Matilda had any childhood memories of her father, King Henry 1 of England, they would have been of a remote and formidable figure, seldom seen. Henry was a ruthless man, sometimes generous, sometimes cruel; he may also have been a murderer.

His brother William Rufus died so conveniently from a chance arrow when hunting in the New Forest that Henry is bound to come under suspicion. *Was* it a chance arrow? Or was it a death meticulously planned? The timing of the death was particularly fortunate for Henry because their older brother, Robert Curthose, was on his way back from the Holy Land and would obviously have had a very good claim to the throne if he had been on the spot when William Rufus died.

Henry was not with William Rufus when he was struck by the arrow, but he was a member of his hunting party and he was near at hand. He did not, however, ride to the place where his brother lay, he did not go to see how he had died or to pay his last respects to his brother's body; on the contrary, he made off at speed to Winchester, where the royal treasure was kept.

Here he ran into trouble. The Treasurer, William de Breteuil, was reluctant to hand over the treasure because he thought Henry's older brother Robert had the better claim. Henry drew his sword in a fury saying that nobody should stand in the way of his rightful inheritance as he was the only son of the Conqueror born 'in the purple'. He got the treasure. Then he rode on to London and three days later he was crowned in Westminster

Abbey. He had not acted a moment too soon for Robert Curthose returned from the Crusade a few weeks later, bringing with him a young wife by whom he might reasonably expect to have children.

Murderer or not, Henry I was a businesslike, effective king; if he broke the law himself, he was quite determined that nobody else should. 'Good man he was and great awe there was of him,' wrote a contemporary. 'No one dared misdo another in his time. Peace he made for man and beast.' He was called the 'Lion of Justice', but perhaps it was orderly government and a well-run country which he loved rather than justice for its own sake, and a well-run country he was determined to have. Crime was incompatible with good order, and when he discovered in 1125 that a 'great quantity of false money' was in circulation because the moneyers had been either clipping the edges of the coins or making them less than the correct weight, he sent for every one of them to come to Winchester. And there, without individual trial to prove guilt or innocence, ninety-four of them were sentenced to have their right hands cut off and to be castrated. Only three men – three moneyers of Winchester – escaped this horrifying punishment; not that the sentence itself was particularly horrifying for the times – punishments of this kind were often inflicted on criminals – but the numbers involved and the cold ruthlessness with which the sentences were carried out did make an impression on contemporaries.

Henry was ruthless in inflicting punishment to achieve an end, but instances of personal cruelty were far rarer. Rebels, however, do seem to have aroused a vicious streak in him and his treatment of the poet Luke de la Barre was considered unnecessarily harsh. There had been a rebellion in support of William Clito, the son of Robert Curthose, and Henry pronounced sentence of blinding on three of the rebels, including Luke de la Barre.

'My lord King,' protested the Count of Flanders, 'these men were fighting in the service of their lords and it is contrary to custom to have them mutilated.'

'I do what is right,' said Henry, 'and I will prove it to you.' Two of the men, he said, had become his liege-men with the consent of their lords and had, in consequence, broken their oaths of fealty by fighting against him. It was true that Luke de la Barre had never paid him homage or made any vow to serve him, but he had been in arms against him once before, and that time Henry had let him go free. He would not do it a second time. What Henry had really found unforgivable was the fact that Luke had dared to write verses making fun of him and had actually sung them in public.

'Now God has delivered him into my hands,' said Henry.

The sentence of blinding was never carried out, however, for Luke fought the men who came to put out his eyes, and then managed to kill himself by dashing his head against the walls of his prison.

On the other hand, Henry treated his brother Robert Curthose with reasonable kindness after defeating him in battle and taking him prisoner. Clearly he could never let him go free to become a focus of rebellion a second time, but he made what concessions he could while keeping him in captivity. It was a long captivity – twenty-eight years. Robert was kept first in Devizes castle, and later in Cardiff, where he passed the time by learning Welsh. He even wrote a sad little poem in Welsh: 'Woe to him that is not old enough to die.'

Henry's love of order extended even to the smallest things and his household was run with strict attention to detail. Everything was predictable, everything was planned. When he went on a journey, all the provisions were ordered in good time so that nobody went short, and the stopping places were precisely indicated – and not changed at the last moment, as happened with other kings – so that everybody had somewhere to sleep. His social arrangements, too, were precise. He talked business with the older and more serious men before dinner, while after dinner he admitted the gayer, younger set. To them he showed quite another side of his character, for he was kind and generous to the young men who were sent to be brought up at his court.

Henry married a few months after he ascended the throne; no doubt he wanted to secure the succession. His bride was Eadgyth, later known as Matilda, the daughter of Malcolm III, King of Scotland, and she was descended from the ancient line of English kings. He was said to have been in love with her for some time, but if so he was unusually lucky in love, for no bride could have been more sensibly chosen. She had been living in Romsey Abbey in the care of her aunt Christina and it was rumoured that she had taken the veil and was therefore not eligible for marriage. The girl herself denied it with passion. She had worn the veil against her will, she said, and then only for protection.

'I trembled under my aunt's rod,' she declared. 'When I threw off the veil, she tormented me and assaulted me with sharp blows and shameful words. I wore it in her presence, groaning and shuddering, but whenever I could get out of her sight, I flung it to the ground and trod it underfoot.'

Anselm, the saintly Archbishop of Canterbury, was asked to investigate the affair and, after going into all the facts thoroughly, he said he was satisfied that she had never been a nun and was free to marry. Moreover, he himself would perform the ceremony.

The new Queen does not seem to have been physically attractive – 'not too bad', said a contemporary. She was, however, very well educated and she had serious literary interests. Since Henry, too, was thought to be learned, he may have sympathised with his wife's desire to make their court a gathering place for erudite men, for poets scholars and musicians; he, however, may have had considerably less sympathy with her extreme piety.

She was formidably pious. She gave generous gifts to religious foundations, but there was nothing out of the way in that; it was much less usual to wear a hair shirt next to the skin in Lent, as the Queen did, and to go barefoot to church – but still such practices were not unheard of. The Queen, however, would go so far as to kiss the ulcers on some poor beggar, press her lips against them even when they were running with pus, and she would touch and fondle lepers. Her brother, David of Scotland, was revolted by her behaviour and spoke to her about it.

'If the King knew,' he told her, 'he would never want to put his lips to yours again.'

'The feet of the eternal King are more precious than the lips of any mortal,' declared the Queen.

Henry might not have been unduly worried if he had never been able to embrace his wife again, for he had plenty of consolation elsewhere. He was considered the most licentious of kings and he is known to have had at least twenty illegitimate children.

Matilda was born to Henry and his Queen in 1102, probably in the second half of the year, but apart from the fact that she had a twin brother, William, virtually nothing is recorded of her childhood. She would have had no settled home, for medieval kings led a nomadic life and seldom spent more than a week or ten days in any one place. The three great courts of the year at which the King wore his crown – Christmas, Easter and Whitsuntide – were generally spent at Gloucester, Winchester and London respectively, but at other times he would journey round the country, staying perhaps at one of his royal castles, or at a hunting lodge, of which he had a good number. Sometimes he would camp out in a rather grand and formal way.

Castle life was relatively luxurious. The great hall was generally on the second floor and there were small side chambers let into the thickness of the wall which were used as bedrooms by the King and the more important of his followers. The floor of the great hall was covered with rushes and there would be a large fireplace with a chimney leading out through the side wall. A fire was needed for most of the year for although the windows were small, they had no glass in them and the cold must often have been intense. The furniture was simple: trestle tables, benches and an occasional heavy chair for people of importance. The food, also, was simple, but for a king, at least, plentiful and reasonably varied. There would be tench, gudgeon, carp and eels from the castle pools; pies, grills and roasts were very popular, sometimes served with heavily spiced sauces; and there would be a good variety of fruit such as peaches, apples, pears and apricots with the occasional addition of creams and sweetmeats. Sugar was virtually unknown, however, and honey was used for sweetening.

Two main meals were served in the day, as a rule, with an occasional snack in between, and dinner was generally enlivened by the playing of minstrels or the recitation of romances to the accompaniment of a harp. Sometimes there might be displays by acrobats or tumblers, and there was nearly always dancing.

Life in a manor house or hunting-lodge was simpler and more congested, for it often consisted of little more than a great hall with a fire in the middle from which the smoke trickled out through a hole in the roof. The King and his family would sleep in the gallery while the servants lay down on the rush-strewn floor below.

Camping scarcely seems the right description of the elaborate arrangements made for the King if he stopped for the night on his travels, for he took virtually all his household with him. A long procession of carts and sumpter-horses would wind along the road after the royal party carrying practically every necessity of daily life. The King's bed and bedding always accompanied him: a fine feather bed with linen sheets, rugs and furs for covering. Tapestries and hangings would be brought as well so that the King might sleep in a suitably dignified setting. On formal journeys the chief officers of his household went with him such as the Chamberlain, who was responsible for the King's bedchamber, his clothes and his jewels; the Steward, who was responsible for the food and drink; and the Chancellor, who was responsible for all records and papers, and was in charge of the Great Seal. He was the highest paid person in the King's service, receiving a daily allowance of five shillings, one loaf of the best quality and two ordinary loaves, one measure of the best wine and one of ordinary wine, one wax candle and forty candle ends. In addition he was entitled to eat at the King's expense and at his table.

Wherever the King stopped on his travels, the place at once became the centre of a great gathering rather like a fair, for merchants flocked from far and wide bringing their goods to sell. Entertainers came too, and there would be sports and amusements such as bear-baiting, cock-fighting and wrestling.

These royal progresses must have been a delight to a child, but

Matilda may very often have been left behind at one or other of the royal residences, and not much notice would have been taken of her when she did accompany the household, for children were largely ignored in those days. It may have been a form of self-protection, for one child in three never lived beyond the age of five. Life was dangerous and harsh with illness, accidents and sheer physical stress to contend with, and only the strong survived.

Matilda would always have had plenty to amuse her. There would have been dolls, tops, toy horses and toy soldiers, and she probably played with knuckle-bones, which were popular at the time. She may have been considered too young as a child to join in the hunting which was the King's passion, but she would have learnt to ride and would have grown up accustomed to the sights and sounds of the chase.

Like his father, William the Conqueror, Henry I preserved the forests and the savage forest laws as rigidly as any king before or after him. The forests were said to be the 'sanctuary and special delight of kings', for there they could lay aside their cares and enjoy a rest from the 'incessant turmoil of the court'. Forests were not, however, the 'special delight' of the men who lived near them in King Henry's time. Game was protected by the harshest laws, and if a deer were killed, an inquest was held on it as though it had been a man, and if the killer were discovered, he might pay with his life. All dogs kept in the neighbourhood of a forest had to be 'lawed' – that is, three claws were cut from their forefeet so that they were unable to pursue game. Even the owners of a forest were not allowed to hunt freely on their own lands.

Henry and his pious Queen, her mind ever on good works, must have seemed rather daunting parents to a small child. Matilda saw little of her father in her early years, however, for he went to Normandy when she was only two years old and he was busy dealing with troubles there for the next three years. She may not have seen much of him even after he came back, for it was probably at about this period that she went away to the Abbey of Wilton to be educated. The nuns would have taught her good manners and the way to conduct herself in society, but perhaps not much else. At this period nuns were not remarkable for their learning, although they would have been competent to teach Matilda to read and write. She may have learnt a little Latin, too, and of course sewing and embroidery. Her education was not entirely entrusted to the nuns, however, for King Henry arranged for Anselm to have a hand in teaching her as well.

She may have spent a fair amount of time in the company of her mother, and perhaps it was at the English court, renowned for its culture and sophistication, that she first acquired a desire to be of importance in the world; but little definite is known of her early childhood. It is tantalising not even to know whether she saw the beginnings of her father's zoo at Woodstock, which later became so famous for its camels and its leopards, its lions and its lynxes, and Henry's favourite exhibit of all, the porcupine presented to him by William of Montpellier.

Matilda was still at an age to play with dolls – or perhaps, being Matilda, she preferred toy soldiers – when envoys arrived from Henry v, who was King of Germany and also, by tradition, Holy Roman Emperor, to ask for her hand in marriage. His envoys came in considerable state and splendour but, even if they had not, they brought an offer which could scarcely be rejected, for the empire included what we now know as Denmark, Holland and Belgium and the Emperor's sphere of influence extended into Italy to just south of Rome, and eastwards over the kingdoms of Poland and Hungary.

Matilda was not yet seven years old, but the offer of marriage was accepted on her behalf by her father and in the spring of 1110, probably before her eighth birthday, she was sent to Germany as the future bride of the Emperor. She took with her an immense dowry, for her father had laid a special tax of three shillings on every hide of land – a hide being about 120 acres – in order to equip her in a style fitting to a future Empress.

Henry v met her at Lüttich and they travelled together to Utrecht where, on 10 April, Matilda was officially betrothed to him. She was too young, of course, for the marriage to be celebrated straight away, but she was crowned Queen at Mainz in

July of the same year. The Archbishop of Mainz had recently died, so Frederick, Archbishop of Cologne, and Bruno, Archbishop of Trier, performed the ceremony, Bruno holding her 'reverently' in his arms.

However excited she was by all this grandeur, Matilda must have suffered at such an abrupt parting with all that she had ever known. Princesses tend to play a sad rôle in history, torn at an early age from their homes, their parents and their countries and sent away to live among strangers; sent away to marry one particular stranger who might, or might not, be to their liking. Matilda was too young to protest, even if she had wanted to, but she cannot have failed to be lonely and frightened when she first went to Germany – the more so as most of her English retinue were dismissed and sent home by the Emperor. He wished her, he said, to learn to speak German as quickly as possible and to become thoroughly German in every way. She was an intelligent child and probably found her lessons no great burden; but what must she have felt as the last of her English companions went away and left her? 'To go from home at the age of eight and into exile for the eternity of three months, in a strange world; it must always be such a parting as will make the other partings of life seem unimportant.'* This was written of a small boy leaving home to go to preparatory school. For Matilda the 'strange world' was a foreign country whose people spoke a tongue she could not understand, and the parting was not for three months, but most likely for life. It may be that the brutality of this early separation from everybody she knew and loved left a permanent mark on her character; and as she came to know something of the reputation of the man she was to marry, she can hardly have felt reassured.

The Emperor Henry v was not yet thirty when he was betrothed to Matilda, but he must have seemed old to her. However, apart from age, she had little to complain about in his outward appearance for, if not particularly handsome, he was reasonably good-looking. He had acquired a sinister reputation, however, for

* *Be Shot for Sixpence* by Michael Gilbert.

a major act of treachery committed against his father, the Emperor Henry IV, a few years before.

Henry IV had had a long-standing quarrel with the Pope over 'investiture' – the practice by which lay monarchs conferred the ring and the staff, the symbols of spiritual office, on newly-appointed bishops and abbots. The Pope, Gregory VII, was determined to put an end to it. 'If an emperor, a king, a duke, a count or any other lay person presumes to give investiture of any ecclesiastical dignity,' he declared, 'let him be excommunicated!' Henry's reaction was spirited. He at once declared the Pope to be deposed – 'no Pope but false monk' – and called on him to leave the position he had 'usurped'. 'Come down, come down!' he called. The Pope retaliated with a sentence of excommunication and a declaration that Henry was no longer Emperor.

It was outright war, but a war that Henry found he could not win, for his subjects were divided and he was soon faced with a revolt on the part of his nobles. In the end, he had to accept complete humiliation. He made a winter journey across the Alps and in January 1077 reached the mountain stronghold of Canossa where the Pope had established himself. For three days he was made to wait outside in the snow and, when at last the Pope admitted him to his presence, he flung himself at the Pope's feet, crying, 'Holy Father, spare me!' The Pope was pleased to be gracious to him and to entertain him at his table, but he said that he himself would decide whether the Emperor might retain his crown or not. In fact, it was the German nobles who decided, for one year later, they chose a new king. Once more Henry found himself excommunicated, and once more he was fighting for his crown.

The future Henry V grew up in the shadow of this struggle between his father and the Pope, and by 1104, he was old enough to take a line of his own. He declared his support for the rebels and put himself at their head. His father was shocked and deeply grieved by this betrayal, and he appealed to him to reconsider what he had done. He could not bear, he said, that his own son should become the instrument of God's vengeance on him for his sins. The young Henry smugly declared that he really did not care to have any contact at all with a man who was excommunicate, actual fighting broke out between them, and the Emperor was put to flight.

His son then sent him a message asking him to meet him at Coblenz so that they might discuss all matters which had a bearing on their mutual 'welfare and honour'. The meeting was an emotional one – genuine emotion on the part of the father, but counterfeit on the part of the prince, who threw himself at his father's feet, begged his forgiveness and made the most solemn and binding promises that for the future he would do all in his power to care for him and protect him from harm. The old Emperor, moved to the heart and with not a thought of treachery, disregarded the warnings of his counsellors and agreed to dismiss his soldiers and go with his son to Mainz. When they were still on the way, however, the young Henry began to make difficulties. It was December and very cold, he said. Perhaps the Bishop of Mainz might refuse to allow his father to enter the city so long as he still lay under sentence of excommunication. Surely it would be wiser and altogether more sensible to turn aside, go quietly into the nearby castle of Bingen and spend Christmas there in 'all honour and peace', while he himself went on to Mainz.

'In the meantime,' he added, 'I shall naturally be doing my utmost to further your interests. I should gladly lay down my life in your cause,' he protested as the Emperor appeared momentarily to hesitate.

The Emperor trustingly went into the castle of Bingen, where he was immediately separated from his own men and surrounded by hostile guards – 'fierce enemies of my life,' as he said later. He was threatened and humiliated – 'swords thrust against my throat if I did not immediately do everything they ordered me' – and was even kept without food. At last a messenger came from his son to tell him that if he did not give up the royal insignia he would be killed. So he parted with his crown, his sceptre, his cross, his lance and his sword, which were sent to his son at Mainz. He was later taken to the village of Ingelheim where, on 31

December 1105, he was forced to abdicate and lay aside with his own hands his remaining emblems of kingship.

'There is nothing I hold more precious than my life,' he said simply. 'Therefore I am bound to do whatever you command.'

For the moment they left him alone, 'despoiled and desolate', but when he received a message from his son instructing him to wait for him at Ingelheim, he fled quickly to Cologne. He knew very well that if he awaited his son's arrival he would be risking imprisonment for life, even if he were not killed.

He was old and he was tired, but he realised that he must once more face the prospect of war with his son. He had some successes at first, but in August 1106 he fell ill and died at Liège. He asked his son to arrange for him to be buried beside his father in the cathedral at Speyer, but Prince Henry took no notice of the request and the Church, carrying vengeance beyond the grave, refused to allow him any Christian burial at all. For five years his body lay in unconsecrated ground at Speyer and it must have been lying there still when Matilda arrived in Germany.

Matilda may have heard nothing of this story of betrayal while she was in England, but if she did, it would have been presented to her in a sympathetic light, for her ultra-pious mother was a supporter of Henry v, seeing him as a champion and defender of Holy Church. If this were so, Matilda did not keep her illusions long, for Henry v was soon quarrelling as heartily with the Pope as had his father before him, and, like his father, he was to spend a fair part of his reign under sentence of excommunication. As Emperor his views on the rights and wrongs of the investiture dispute underwent a radical change, and in August 1110, only a few months after the arrival of Matilda, he set off for Rome to demand a confirmation of his rights from the Pope. He left Matilda at the royal residence in Speyer in the company of Archbishop Bruno of Trier, who had been very kind to Matilda and was in large part responsible for her education.

Pope Paschal ii became increasingly nervous as Henry and his army approached Rome – so much so that he offered a compromise. He could not, he said, consent to lay investiture or give up

the right to free canonical election to vacant sees, but if the
Emperor would agree to these reservations, he, on his side, would
renounce all the Church's secular property – its lands, its treasure
and all its vast possessions. All that the princes of the Church
would have left would be their tithes and their offerings. There
was one exception: the huge possessions of the Roman See were
not to be included in this sweepingly handsome offer.

Henry accepted (he would have been mad not to do so) and on
12 February 1111 he presented himself at St Peter's for the
traditional hallowing of the Emperor by the Pope. Before the
ceremony began, however, the agreement was read out, and
immediately violence and tumult erupted on every side. The
bishops and abbots, in particular, were outraged at the off-hand
way in which the Pope was prepared to give away their property
while carefully safeguarding his own. The brawling spread to the
streets and Henry took advantage of the wild scenes to kidnap
the Pope and drag him by force to his camp outside the city.
Paschal was held captive for two months, but at last he capitu-
lated: Henry might appoint bishops at will and invest them with
staff and ring.

'For the peace and liberty of the Church,' said Paschal, 'I am
compelled to do what I would never have done to save my own
life.'

Henry was crowned by the Pope in St Peter's on 12 April and
returned home in triumph. An incidental result of his success was
the fact that his father was at last buried, as he had wished,
beside his own father in the cathedral at Speyer.

Matilda, busy at her lessons in Germany, can hardly have
escaped hearing of the startling events taking place in Rome, for
even lay opinion was deeply shocked by what had happened.
How shocked was she herself? She had had a strictly religious
upbringing and she may have been terrified at the thought of
being married to a man who had laid violent hands on the Pope.
It would be natural; but there was nothing she could do except go
on with her lessons and hope that her future would not be too
unhappy.

She was married three years later, on either 6 or 7 June 1114, when she was not yet twelve. The wedding was a brilliant affair attended by a number of foreign princes as well as five dukes, five archbishops and thirty bishops. There were singers and jugglers and dancers gathered from all over the country. Everything was provided, in fact, to make the celebrations as splendid and festive as possible. Henry, usually so sombre and withdrawn, showered gifts on everybody and made a great impression by his generosity. Matilda, too, made an impression. In spite of her youth, she was dignified and gracious, and succeeded in making herself liked by all their high-born guests and the people at large.

Against all probability, she made a success of her marriage as well. She cannot have found Henry an agreeable companion for he was by no means a cheerful sinner and was subject to fits of gloomy remorse, particularly about his betrayal of his father. Yet somehow or other, over the years, they achieved a degree of understanding. She was not very often in his company, for sporadic revolts kept breaking out in Germany, often fomented by churchmen who disapproved of Henry's attitude to the Church; the country, in fact, was hardly ever at peace. However, in 1116 Henry went to Italy again and this time Matilda went with him. They stayed at a number of places on the way – in January they were at Worms, in February at Augsburg and in early March they crossed the Alps and went to stay in the Doge's Palace in Venice. After that, they travelled on by slow stages to Rome, where they arrived in January 1117.

Henry spent the next year in renewed conflict with the Pope and this time Matilda was a spectator of the struggle at first hand. Henry had made up his mind to be crowned in Rome a second time, but the Pope, deeply unhappy at the prospect of seeming to give approval to an enemy of the Church, fled to a safe distance. Henry, not to be defeated, found a substitute in the person of Maurice, Archbishop of Braga, who performed the ceremony and was promptly excommunicated; so was Henry.

Matilda should have been shocked and upset at finding herself married to an excommunicate; a man, moreover, who completely ignored the sentence and gave support to an anti-Pope. According to all that she had been taught, it was wrong to have any contact at all with a man under sentence of excommunication, and if such a man should ¡die, his soul, so she had been told, would fly at once to hell to endure the ghastly torments so horrifyingly described by medieval writers for 'as many thousands of years as there are drops in the sea'. Matilda, however, showed no sign of distress; on the contrary, at fifteen years old, she was thoroughly enjoying her first taste of adult responsibility. She took a share in the business of government and even acted as her husband's personal representative at local assemblies. In September, for instance, she settled a dispute concerning some property between Bishop Hugo of Reggio and another man. She seems also to have been able to exercise a degree of influence over her husband, for it was at about this time that she persuaded him to confer the See of Verdun on a former Archdeacon of Winchester, one of the very few members of her English retinue who had been allowed to stay on in Germany.

When the Emperor was obliged to return to Germany to deal with some troubles there, Matilda remained in Italy, virtually as Governor, and in the only charter which has survived from this period, she is seen once again in court, this time presiding over a case concerning the theft of church property.

In 1119 she followed Henry back to Germany, where he was still busy putting down a series of insurrections, and she was with him most of the time for the next three years. It is just possible that she paid a visit to England in 1122, and if so, her visit may have had some bearing on the treaty which was made soon afterwards between Henry I and the Emperor. Henry I had been having trouble with his Norman barons and the Emperor, to prevent Louis of France from intervening, massed his forces on the Rhine. Supporters flocked to the French King, however, and the ¡Emperor's army was defeated; Henry I tartly advised his son-in-law to hire some mercenaries to fight for him in future.

The Emperor returned from the campaign in poor health, and during the stormy winter of 1124-5 he became seriously ill. None the less, he was with Matilda at Duisburg in May, and at her request he made grants to the Abbey of St Maximin at Trier, of which she had affectionate memories dating back to her early days in Germany when she had often visited it in the company of Archbishop Bruno.

They spent Whitsuntide at Utrecht, but Henry's illness grew worse and it became clear that he was dying. He set about making the usual lavish bequests to the Church in penitence for the sins of his life, and on 22 May 1125 he died. He was not quite forty-four years old. Matilda was with him during his illness and it seems that at the very least he trusted her, for almost his last act was to place the insignia of royalty in her hands; he may even have loved her. German writers of the time praised her for her 'prudent and gracious behaviour' to her husband, and she was popular with his German subjects; but in one respect, perhaps the most important of all, she had been a failure. She had borne her husband no child; he left behind him no heir. It is not known whether he ever reproached her but she would not have needed reproaches to be aware of a failure which must have grown more bitter to her with every year. Popular opinion, however, did not blame her, for their childlessness was regarded as a punishment from God for Henry's cruel treatment of his father.

Matilda was twenty-two years old and a widow. She was no longer Empress – in fact, she had the chagrin of seeing her husband's throne pass to an enemy of his house. She had lost her former power and importance and although she was still welcome in Germany her circumstances were greatly changed.

Her situation had also been affected by a disaster which had taken place five years before – the loss of the White Ship, which occurred off Barfleur in December 1120. Henry I was returning from Normandy to England when Prince William decided to sail with a party of young men in a ship of their own, the White Ship. The King put to sea, but William stayed on shore drinking and he saw to it that his crew, also, was well supplied with barrels of wine. Darkness was falling when at last they put to sea, hilarious and very drunk, and as they were leaving harbour, the ship was dashed against a rock. It was badly holed and began to sink. Their cries for help could be clearly heard in the darkness, but it was impossible to see what had happened. The ship quickly settled in the water and went down with all on board – all, that is, except for one man. He was a butcher from Rouen who swam all through the night, clinging to a broken mast, and came ashore in the morning. He brought the first news of the disaster.

There was another man who had a lucky escape, and that was Stephen of Blois, the King's nephew. He was to have sailed in the White Ship, but changed his mind at the last moment because he was so disgusted by the drunken behaviour of the prince's party. According to another account, he was suffering from diarrhoea and did not feel well enough to sail.

It was a dreadful blow for the King, for he had lost not only his one legitimate son, but two other children as well, born out of wedlock, and very many friends. According to popular legend, 'he never smiled again'.

Henry was left with no heir to succeed him, for Matilda, as the wife of the Emperor, would not have been acceptable to the barons. So he married a second time in the hope of having children, chosing as his wife Adelisa, the strikingly beautiful daughter of the Duke of Louvain; but she was childless.

Four years later, when the Emperor died and Matilda became a widow, Henry decided to seize the opportunity to make her heir to the throne. The first thing, of course, was to bring her back from Germany, and he sent for her to join him in Normandy, where he happened to be at the time. Matilda was far from pleased. Germany had been her country since she was seven years old, and German was now her first language. She thought as a German and had become accustomed to German ways. Moreover, she was popular in Germany. She was known to her German subjects as the 'good Matilda', the 'virtuous Matilda', and when they heard they were to lose her, they begged her to stay. As for England, after fifteen years of absence, it had become like a foreign land to her. As the King's heir, she would have more importance in England than she would in Germany as the Emperor's widow, but this was not enough to console her for the bitterness of leaving the country she had made her own. There was nothing, however, that she could do. She was a grown woman and as Empress she had exercised considerable authority on her own account, yet now she was scarcely more in control of her destiny than she had been when she first went to Germany at seven years old.

An escort was sent by her father, the King, to bring her to Normandy and, since they were unable to stop her leaving, a number of German nobles accompanied her on the journey so as to make a personal appeal to her father to allow her to stay with them in Germany. But he would not hear of it; Matilda was his only legitimate child and he had made up his mind that she was to inherit his throne.

Matilda remained in Normandy with her father for nearly a year and became very friendly with her step-mother, Queen Adelisa, who, for her part, was probably glad to have a young companion. Henry by this time was inclined to be morose and gloomy, and he was plagued by nightmares in which farmers threatened him with pitchforks and knights rushed at him with drawn swords. He would often leap out of bed in the middle of the night and seize a weapon to defend himself.

They set sail for England in the late summer of 1126, Matilda bringing her possessions with her. She had had to leave behind her in Germany a good part of the magnificent dowry bestowed on her by the Emperor, but she did have one distinctly unusual item in her luggage: she brought with her to England the hand of St James the Apostle.

2 The Angevin Connection👃

The English court was livelier and more relaxed than the German court; in fact, the historian William of Malmesbury thought it positively licentious. He particularly disapproved of the way men dressed to look like women, 'forgetting what they were born'. They wore their hair as long, if not longer than women, and if their own hair was getting thin, they wore wigs. There is no reason to suppose, however, that Henry's court was not perfectly well-behaved at this time. He had had a record number of mistresses in his day, but he was growing old and he had, in any case, a beautiful young wife.

Matilda must have found her new life distinctly pleasant. She would have enjoyed the hunting and hawking perhaps as much as her father did, and after living in a country almost constantly at war, the gaiety of medieval life in England with its endless round of fairs and travelling spectacles must have given her great pleasure. Above all, after being used to the company of a harsh-tempered husband old enough to be her father, she found herself surrounded by a group of lively young men who had become her father's protégés for one reason or another. There were the twin sons of Henry I's old friend the Count of Meulan, who were not only lively but exceptionally brilliant. There was Brian fitzCount, the natural son of Alan Fergant, Count of Brittany, an intelligent and well-educated man of considerable charm. Most important of all, there was her cousin Stephen of Blois, the 'handsomest man in Europe'.

Stephen was a grandson of William the Conqueror through his

mother Adela, who was a remarkable woman, intrepid and determined, a true child of the Conqueror. She was also exceptionally well-educated as well as beautiful, and would have liked to be a warrior like her father; she would probably have made a good fighter – far better than her husband, Stephen of Blois, with whom she was unequally yoked.

Stephen of Blois was a good-natured, home-loving man who must have found his formidable wife something of a trial. It would have been difficult to live up to her at the best, and Stephen had bad luck. Ordinarily brave in war, he committed one notorious act of cowardice which left a permanent stain on his reputation.

He joined the First Crusade in 1096 and in the beginning he was a great success. 'All our leaders,' he wrote to his wife, 'by the common consent of the whole army, have appointed me – though I did not want it – their lord and commander-in-chief.' The Crusaders captured Nicaea and then went on to take the city of Antioch after a prolonged siege. The Turks, however, continued to hold out in the citadel, and soon the Crusaders found themselves besieged in their turn, for a large army of Turks advanced on the city and surrounded it. Stephen lost heart, his health began to fail, or so he said, and he went off to Alexandretta to recuperate.

The Crusaders, left behind to continue the struggle at Antioch, waited impatiently for their leader to recover and come back to them. They were suffering severe privations, with little food or supplies of any kind, and they were making no progress against the vast armies of the Turks, so vast that they 'covered the plains like the sand on the sea-shore'. Stephen caught a glimpse of these armies from the top of a hill near his retreat at Alexandretta and was appalled. He hurried back to his fortress, packed his belongings and fled for the coast without wasting a minute. On the way, he met the Emperor Alexius of Constantinople who was advancing to the relief of the Crusaders with a powerful army at his back. Stephen told him that it was too late. The Turks had taken the city by assault and put the Christians to the sword. 'Look to your own safety!' he called, and so persuaded the Emperor to turn back.

Thanks to Stephen, their elected leader, the Crusaders were left to their fate. It should have been the end for them, but in fact they won an unexpected victory which proved to be the turning-point of the whole campaign; but Stephen, their commander, was not with them.

He had made for home with all possible speed, but when he arrived, his welcome was lukewarm. Adela was not a wife to take kindly to a husband who was branded as a coward. She tried to inspire him with her own iron courage, she gave him no peace, and constantly she demanded that he wipe out his shame by returning to the Holy Land. Even in the marriage bed, in the midst of an embrace, she would whisper, 'Show a little courage! Take up arms in a noble cause!'

Home, clearly, was no longer the place of peace and refuge Count Stephen had pictured when he was far away on Crusade. He was, by inclination, a domesticated, quiet-living sort of man, but his wife was determined that he should be a hero. In the end, he could resist his fate no longer and knowing but too well what was before him, he set out – reluctantly – once more on Crusade. He did well at the beginning, as he had done before. With his fellow Crusaders, he marched through Asia Minor and reached Jerusalem in time to celebrate Easter there in 1102. He had entered the Holy City, he had restored his credit, and now, surely, he could return home to a less critical family. He made his way to Joppa and was just about to set sail when a call came to join in repelling an army of the infidels which was advancing against the Crusaders. With a sad heart, he turned back. Battle was joined, Stephen fought with great courage; and was killed.

He was scarcely missed at home. Adela, consoled in her widowhood by having had an acknowledged hero for a husband, was well able to play any masculine rôle demanded of her. She was now in charge of their five sons and three daughters, and she disposed of them with quick competence. The daughters presented no difficulty, and suitable husbands were soon found for them. The eldest son was a problem, and she dealt with him ruthlessly. He was simply not equipped to play the part of eldest son, although it is not clear whether his failings were physical, mental or moral; but in some way he was inadequate. So he was pushed firmly aside, settled with a reasonably suitable wife, and it was the second son, Theobald, who succeeded to his father's titles and lands.

Adela evidently felt that the best she could do for Stephen, her third son, was to send him to be brought up at the court of his powerful uncle, Henry I. Henry received him with great kindness, lavished presents on him and later arranged an exceedingly advantageous marriage for him to the heiress of Count Eustace III of Boulogne, who was also a granddaughter of the King of Scotland. She brought him not only Boulogne but large estates in England as well, and these, together with the lands which Stephen had already received from the King, made Stephen one of the richest men in England.

Adela decided that her fourth son, Henry, should go into the Church; so he was sent to the Abbey of Cluny when he was still a child. He grew into a brilliant, truly exceptional man and in 1126 his uncle, the King, made him Abbot of Glastonbury. Three years later he was created Bishop of Winchester as well, so that he became as rich as, if not richer, than his brother Stephen. From these positions of power, he wielded a formidable influence on English affairs for the next forty years.

The last son, Philip, also entered the Church and eventually became Bishop of Chalons, but he played no major part in public affairs. As for Adela herself, her work complete, she retired to the Cluniac Priory of Marcigny, where she spent the remaining years of her life.

Even Adela, ambitious as she was for her children, probably never entertained the idea that Stephen might one day claim the English throne, and King Henry certainly never thought of such a thing, for he was determined to establish Matilda as his heir. This was not going to be easy. In the first place, his elder brother, Robert Curthose, was still alive, though in captivity. Nobody would have been likely to press his claim to the throne, even if he were free, for he had always been feckless and unreliable and, when he was Duke of Normandy, he had been treated with so little respect by his followers that sometimes he could not get up in the morning because they had gone off with his clothes. Robert had a son, however, William Clito – or William the Prince – who was far more dangerous. He clearly had a claim to the throne, in some ways a better claim than Matilda since he was the eldest son of the eldest son of the Conqueror. Henry had tried to seize William when he was a child, but he had been hidden away by friends of his father; he was therefore still at large and causing trouble.

Henry decided that the best way to ensure Matilda's succession was to persuade the leading men of the realm to swear a solemn oath, while he was still alive, to accept her as their ruler after his death. He knew that it would not be a popular move for there were obvious drawbacks to having a woman on the throne. At a time when force played a large part in the settlement of affairs a woman was clearly at a disadvantage. Moreover in the feudal system a woman had virtually no standing on her own but was dependent in most things on her nearest male relative or overlord. Above all, there was the question of who her husband was to be, for although he might not have any official standing, it was accepted that he would be the ruler in practice. A husband from their own ranks would provoke envy and rivalry, but a husband from a foreign country to lord it over them would be even worse. Also, as Henry well knew, a number of the barons favoured William Clito in any case.

Henry broached the question of the succession at his Christmas court of 1126–7. He spoke first of the unhappy blow of fate which had taken from him his only son William, who would otherwise have come to the throne after him. None the less, he still had a daughter who happily was alive and had come back to England to live amongst them. She was the legitimate descendant of kings. Her grandfather William the Conqueror, her uncle William Rufus and he, her father, had all ruled England before her.

B

And she was the descendant of kings on her mother's side as well; of fourteen kings, no less, beginning with Egbert, King of the West Saxons in the ninth century, and going right on to Edward the Confessor, whose remains lay buried at Westminster. She was, he maintained, his rightful heir and it was she who should rule in his place when he was dead. He called on them to make a solemn vow to accept her as their Queen at his death 'without delay or hesitation'.

First to take the oath was William, Archbishop of Canterbury, followed by the other leading churchmen of the kingdom. David, King of Scotland, Matilda's uncle, had the obvious claim to first place among the laymen, and he took his oath next; but then a dispute sprang up as to who had the right to make his vow after him. Robert of Gloucester, the eldest of the King's natural sons, claimed it, but so also did Stephen, the King's nephew. Stephen won the argument and made his solemn vow to accept Matilda as his future queen. After him, all the other nobles of the kingdom made the same vow.

Matilda was much too realistic to imagine she was now sure of the succession, but such a vow, publicly sworn, was a serious matter, and a broken vow involved perjury. At the very least the ceremony gave her position at Court an added importance, which she must have enjoyed. Succession to the throne, however, was a fairly remote contingency and she was probably more occupied with the pleasures of the moment, and with the looming shadows of her immediate future. The pleasures of the moment included her cousin Stephen, who was living at Court. There was some gossip about their relationship at the time and it is possible that they may have been lovers. It would have been natural enough for her to find him attractive, for he was not only good-looking but also a man of great charm, who could always make himself liked. But the future meant the marriage she would certainly have to make soon. The question was, to whom? To what sort of man? Stephen, of course, could not be considered since he was already married.

She was highly eligible; she knew that there would be many

men wanting to marry her and that she would have little or no
say in the final choice. Henry I may have loved his only daughter,
but even if he did, his affection would not, and did not, extend to
considering her feelings about so important a subject as marriage.
In the event, her father's chosen bridegroom turned out to be far
worse, from her point of view, than anything she could possibly
have imagined.

The French King Louis VI had always been unhappy about the
fact that Normandy and England were united under one ruler,
and he welcomed any chance of forcing a wedge between the two
by promoting the claims of William Clito. Fulk, Count of Anjou,
was also inclined to support William Clito, because of the long
hereditary enmity between Normandy and Anjou. This had been
temporarily patched up by the marriage which had taken place
between Fulk's elder daughter, Matilda, and Henry's only
legitimate son William, but William's death had dissolved these
ties and Fulk later married his younger daughter Sibyl to William
Clito. Henry managed to get the marriage annulled by the Pope
on the grounds of consanguinity, but Louis of France countered
this move by giving William Clito his wife's half-sister Jeanne in
marriage, and presenting her with the Vexin, the land which lies
on the borders of Normandy north of the Seine, as her dowry.

The support given to William Clito by the King of France and
the Count of Anjou, and William's increasing power and influence,
had become a major problem to Henry. It was this, and the
chance of breaking up the alliance between his two old enemies,
France and Anjou, which prompted his choice of a match for
Matilda – a match which might otherwise have seemed a little
beneath her dignity. The Count of Anjou had an unmarried son,
Geoffrey; Henry had an unmarried daughter, Matilda. So what
more suitable than to arrange a marriage between them?
Especially as a new link between England and Anjou would
deprive William Clito of a large part of his support.

To Matilda, the proposal was quite simply an outrage. In later
life, she was described as haughty and arrogant, and pride may
have been a natural trait of her character. If so, it would have been

nourished by her position as Empress and the stiff etiquette of the German Court. But even the meekest of women might have resented being asked to exchange an Emperor for the son of a Count. And there was worse still: Geoffrey was a mere boy – he was not yet fourteen – while she was nearly twenty-five. She was a woman of the world who had acted for the Emperor in important affairs, she was an acknowledged beauty and she was, moreover, the heir to the English throne. What was he in comparison?

She rebelled against the marriage as far as she was able. She argued, she stormed, and it was said that Henry had to shut her up in her room and make her virtually a prisoner before she would give in, as of course she had to in the end. She had no effective weapons to use against her father. He had the right to betroth her to whomsoever he chose and he intended to do so. The barons might have been on her side if she could have appealed to them, for they were certain to dislike an alliance between Matilda, the heir to the throne, and an Angevin Count, but Henry, realising this, kept his plans to himself until the ceremony of betrothal took place.

Matilda was sent to Normandy in the spring of 1127 in the care of her half-brother Robert of Gloucester and Brian fitzCount; her father followed a little later. The marriage did not take place at once, however, for the bridegroom was considered to be too young, but Henry made him a knight with full pomp and ceremony. Indeed he seems to have gone out of his way to be particularly friendly to the young man, perhaps to counterbalance the sour looks from his daughter. She was not, it seems, mollified by Geoffrey's exceptional good looks; he was nicknamed 'the Handsome' and apparently deserved the title. And he had more than looks to offer. He was intelligent and so well-educated that he was able to sustain serious conversation with the scholarly Henry I. It was even said that he would have been able to carry on the conversation in Latin, if he had chosen. He was interested in literature and the arts, and it was later said of him that he had such a passionate interest in history, 'all battles fought, all great deeds done', that he never rode out to war without a scholar at his side. In war, he was to show himself a reasonably brave and capable leader though neither reckless nor showy. The chief defect of his character was a certain essential cold-heartedness, but that would not have been apparent on such brief acquaintance.

The marriage took place in June 1128 at Le Mans, where Geoffrey and Matilda spent three weeks in feasting and celebration before going on to Angers, where they were greeted with peals of bells, processions of priests with lighted tapers, the singing of hymns and every kind of rejoicing. Geoffrey's mother was dead and his father went off to Jerusalem almost at once in order to marry the daughter of the King of Jerusalem, so the young couple were left to themselves. Matilda's anger at the match and her total inability to prevent it seem to have boiled up to such a pitch that she made no attempt to behave with reasonable restraint. She behaved, in fact, so outrageously to her boy husband that Geoffrey, who even at fifteen had considerable character, refused to tolerate it any longer. He packed her off to Normandy after not much more than a year of marriage with a humiliatingly small retinue. She took refuge in Rouen, and from there bombarded her father with letters of complaint about the insulting way in which she had been treated.

Henry did not hurry to her support. He was no doubt angry at the setback to his plans, especially as Matilda's position as heir to the throne had been unexpectedly strengthened by the death of her rival William Clito in 1128 as the result of a wound. He must also have suspected that the apparent breakdown of the marriage was more the fault of his daughter than of his son-in-law. Accordingly, he took his time before responding to Matilda's appeals. He did join her in Normandy eventually, however, and he brought her back with him to England in 1131. Once there, it seemed a good idea to take the opportunity of getting the barons to make a second vow to accept her as his heir. This was done at a Council held in Northampton in September 1131, and once more her cousin Stephen was amongst the first to make his vow. It seemed that his loyalty and his enthusiasm in her support knew no bounds.

Geoffrey had meanwhile been busy fighting off a revolt in his own lands, but by this time he had succeeded in establishing order; he had also begun to realise that he had been rather hasty in sending Matilda away, for she was, after all, an important heiress and a potential asset as a wife. He therefore made a formal application to King Henry asking that she might return to him, and it was decided at the Council of Northampton that his request should be granted. So Matilda set off once more for Anjou. It is not known whether she was pleased or not, but at least she made no resistance.

The reunion, if not rapturous, was this time realistic. The experience of war during the preceding years had turned Geoffrey from a boy into a man, and he had learnt to control his temper. For her part, Matilda had no wish to experience a second time all the humiliations of a cast-off wife and she was prepared to try and make the marriage work. On 5 March 1133 their first child, the future King Henry II, was born. Matilda wept at his baptism, the only time she was ever known to shed tears. His birth had at last wiped out the long shame of her failure to bear a child while she was Empress, and to the end of her life she loved Henry dearly.

Her father loved him too. He was, in fact, quite delighted with his little grandson, partly perhaps because his own second marriage had brought him no children. He lived to see Matilda's second son, Geoffrey, born as well, but there were complications after his birth which brought Matilda near to death. As she lay apparently dying, she asked that her body might be buried in the Abbey of Bec, for which she had a particular affection, but her father disagreed and said it would be more fitting for her to be buried in Rouen. The argument was still unsettled when she unexpectedly recovered, much to the relief of the monks of Bec, who by this time were 'fainting and ready to expire under the burden of their ceaseless prayers for their benefactress'.

Henry I had grown gloomier with the passing of the years; he had never fully recovered his spirits since the drowning of his son in the disaster of the White Ship. His young grandson, however,

gave him so much pleasure that he spent almost all of the remaining two years of his life in Normandy, chiefly at his palace
near Rouen, leaving his Justiciar, Roger of Salisbury, to manage
affairs in England. Henry II used to speak of his grandfather with
great affection in later years, though whether he can really have
remembered much about him is doubtful.

Matilda spent the greater part of these years at her father's
court in Normandy, where Geoffrey visited her from time to time,
but his visits only brought quarrels. He made claim to some
castles in Normandy, maintaining that Henry had promised them
to him at his marriage, but Henry refused angrily, saying that as
long as he lived he had no intention of making anyone his equal
in his own house. Geoffrey lost patience, and in the spring of
1135 he launched a series of attacks on towns and castles in
Normandy. This in turn so infuriated the King that he talked of
taking Matilda to England with him. Her own attitude to the
quarrel is a little obscure. There is some evidence that she tried to
act as a peacemaker between her husband and her father, but if so,
she certainly had no success, and in the end she went with her
two children to join her husband, apparently without taking any
leave of her father.

She never saw him again. By December he was dead, killed, so
it was said, by a 'surfeit of lampreys', a delicacy which disagreed
with him and which he had been advised never to eat again. He
had been out hunting near Rouen, but was taken ill in the night
and died five days later, on 1st December 1135, after making his
confession to Hugh, Archbishop of Rouen. At his bedside were
gathered his natural son Robert of Gloucester, Waleran of
Meulan and his twin brother Robert of Leicester, William de
Warenne and Rotrou of Mortain. Although his daughter was not
there, Henry is said to have declared her to be his heir, leaving
her all his territories on both sides of the Channel in 'legitimate
and perpetual succession'. Her husband he did not mention.

Henry had been a harsh ruler in some respects, but he had been
efficient and businesslike, and he had at least established the rule
of law in his lands. He may not have made himself particularly

popular in his lifetime, but after his death, men looked back on his reign as to a golden age, for he had governed his territories in 'great peace and prosperity' as a contemporary said of him, 'and every man's house was his castle'.

It was to be very different in the years that followed.

3 Who Shall Rule?

'God grant him peace, for peace he loved,' wrote the Archbishop of Rouen at Henry's death; but on earth his death was the signal for conflict. Stephen sprang into action at once with all the appearance of carrying out a long-prepared plan, a plan so well-conceived, in fact, that it seems likely that it had been devised by his highly intelligent brother Henry, Bishop of Winchester.

Stephen was at Boulogne when he heard the news, and he sailed at once for England with only a few companions. The winds were favourable and he landed at Dover without mishap, but here his reception was discouraging, for the castellan of the castle would have nothing to do with him. The city of Canterbury was equally unwelcoming and refused to let him inside the gates, so he hurried on to London, still accompanied by only a few followers; and there he did better. He was received with enthusiasm by the leading citizens, who proceeded to call a general assembly at which he was 'elected' king. Of course they had no formal right to make any such election, but they had a great deal of influence. They seem to have made some sort of pact with Stephen by which he swore that he would 'gird himself with all his might to keep the kingdom at peace' while they promised to support him with money and by force of arms.

With London behind him, Stephen travelled quickly on to Winchester, where the royal treasure was kept. It was of vast proportions after years of careful management by Henry I and Stephen felt that if he could only get possession of it, most of his practical problems would be solved. Here, however, he

encountered the first serious hitch in his plans. His brother
Henry came out to meet him at the head of the citizens, but the
Treasurer, William de Pont de l'Arche, at first made difficulties
about accepting Stephen's authority. The backing of Bishop
Henry was decisive, however, and Stephen gained possession of
his uncle's treasure.

The next most important step was to secure recognition from
the leading churchmen and nobles of the kingdom – chief among
them, of course, William de Corbeil, Archbishop of Canterbury,
who alone had the right to crown him king. His consent was not
given easily. He was troubled by the recollection of the oath
which he, and Stephen himself, had sworn to recognise Matilda
as Henry's successor. To break it would surely be perjury.
Bishop Henry and Stephen's other supporters argued, however,
that the oath had been exacted under duress and was therefore
not binding.

Roger, Bishop of Salisbury, produced another argument to
excuse the breaking of the oath. He said that it had been conditional; conditional on Matilda not being given in marriage to
any man outside the kingdom without the consent of the Great
Council. It is highly unlikely that anybody had the courage to
attempt to lay down conditions to Henry at the time, and the
reservation, if it ever existed, must have been in the mind alone.
Roger's support was vital to Stephen, for he was not merely a
bishop, but as Henry's Justiciar – that is, his chief minister who
had acted as Regent in his absence overseas – he was probably the
single most powerful man in the country after the King.

His association with Henry had begun some time before he
became King. Henry had come across him by chance, almost
certainly at a church near Caen, where Roger was a priest. He made
an instant impression on Henry by the speed at which he said
mass. 'Just the priest for a soldier!' exclaimed Henry and at once
attached him to his retinue. As soon as Henry became King,
Roger rose rapidly in power and importance, for he was a man of
unusual business capacity and he was prepared to work hard; and
if he became immensely rich as well, Henry had no objection.

Roger was an enthusiastic builder and he built, among other things, the cathedral at Old Sarum. He also built a great castle at Devizes, amongst the finest in Europe, and another at Sherborne. He was, in fact, an outstanding example of the worldly prelate, so disapproved of by the future St Bernard of Clairvaux, for by far the greater part of his time under Henry I must have been devoted to secular business. Outstandingly successful, influential and important as he had been, he was now in the slightly vulnerable position of having lost his patron. He needed another; but it was vital to choose the right one.

He went over to Stephen. Stephen had, after all, a good claim as the grandson of the Conqueror. True, it was through the female line; but then Matilda was a woman, so where was the difference? Besides, Stephen was the man on the spot, and he looked like succeeding. There was the matter of the vow, of course, but Roger had already seen his way out of that difficulty.

And then, providentially as it seemed, Hugh Bigod, Earl of Norfolk, appeared on the scene in the classic rôle of the surprise witness. He brought the startling news that the King had changed his mind on his deathbed and regretted the oath he had forced on his barons to recognise Matilda. He had disinherited her and had made Stephen his heir instead. This was indeed dramatic news, but Hugh Bigod swore an oath before the Archbishop of Canterbury that what he said was the truth; and he was believed. It seemed a happy stroke of fortune; except that it was almost certainly a lie. In the first place, he had not been present when Henry I died, and his story was not borne out by those who were. Robert of Gloucester, who *was* present, later called Hugh Bigod a perjurer, and the others who were there, including men who were Stephen's friends, did not come forward to support his story. Furthermore, the Archbishop of Rouen, in writing to the Pope to inform him of Henry's death, made no mention of what would surely have been an interesting piece of information. More significantly still, the Norman nobles had immediately offered the crown to Theobald of Blois, Stephen's elder brother, which they would scarcely have done if Henry had made Stephen his heir.

When the news came that Stephen was already in England and had claimed the crown, Theobald made a graceful withdrawal.

There is also the question of probability. Henry had gone to great lengths to try to secure the succession to Matilda, which suggests that it was important to him that his crown should descend in the direct line. It is true that he was angry with Matilda at the time of his death and that her husband was in more or less open revolt against him; but on the other hand he had been more than usually devoted to his young grandson and it seems unlikely that he would have done anything to disinherit him.

There is no evidence as to whether Hugh Bigod's story had been concocted in advance as a means of strengthening Stephen's position, or whether it was a happy inspiration of the moment. Its plausibility depended, of course, on the chance that Matilda was not at her father's side when he died; also that it was known that she was on bad terms with him. None the less, prudence, if not natural affection, might have brought her hurrying to him when she heard the news of his illness. Perhaps the story had been prepared to use, or not to use, as circumstances dictated.

On balance, Stephen was probably the most welcome choice to the majority of the barons, given that none of them wanted a woman. As against Theobald, his elder brother, he was a known and familiar figure who had passed most of his life in England, while Theobald was a stranger to most of them. He was also an attractive figure, superficially at least. He was dashing and gallant, warm-hearted, friendly and generous. He was also kind, but in promises only, said William of Malmesbury. Performance was quite another matter. His easy manners had made him popular with the people as a whole, for he was a good mixer, ready to chat and joke with anybody. His chief weakness was a lack of resolution and method, and later events were to prove him untrustworthy.

At this period of history, kinship, or direct inheritance, was only one of the factors in determining who should be king. Neither of the two preceding kings, William Rufus and Henry I, had been the obvious heirs. Their elder brother Robert had been

alive when each of them had succeeded; but they were, on the
other hand, both of the royal blood, and that had importance.
The wishes of the preceding ruler were regarded as important, too,
but in this case the picture was blurred. Henry I had extracted
solemn oaths from his barons that Matilda should succeed him,
but had he changed his mind on his deathbed? The other important factor was the candidate himself and his suitability to be
king. Here Matilda, as a woman, was at a grave disadvantage,
and her Angevin husband did her no service. No Norman would
choose to be ruled by an Angevin, and it was assumed that her
husband would be the effective ruler if she were Queen. Above
all, Stephen was there, ready to take over, and a period of inter-
regnum, with all the upheavals it would be likely to involve,
would be avoided if they accepted him.

So nobody felt inclined to raise serious objections to Stephen's
claim to be king, and it only remained for the Church to wring
from him some sort of undertaking as to his future behaviour in
ecclesiastical affairs. The Archbishop, in particular, demanded
that he should make an oath to restore and maintain the liberties
of the Church, an oath which was to be made in a more detailed
and specific form after he was recognised by the Pope. Stephen
agreed, Henry of Winchester stood surety for his good faith, and
the matter was settled. The Archbishop of Canterbury anointed
Stephen king on 22 December 1135, but very few of the magnates
of the Kingdom attended the coronation – only three bishops, no
abbots at all and a sprinkling of nobles.

His position was now immeasurably more secure, however, for
the act of anointing was more than a confirmation of his claim; it
was held to have the power actually to make a king. Stephen had
certainly achieved much in a bare three weeks. It was, perhaps,
the one thoroughly successful achievement of his life.

Meanwhile, the man whose death had set all these events in
train was still awaiting burial. Henry's body had been taken first
of all to Rouen where, in a quiet part of the cathedral church, the
bowels, brain and eyes were removed so that the body should not
smell too offensive. These remains were then buried in the

monastery of Notre Dame des Prés near Rouen, while his body was taken on to Caen. There it remained for nearly a month as the weather was too stormy for a crossing to be made, and it was after Christmas before his body was at last put on board ship and taken to England. He was buried at Reading on 4 January 1136 in the abbey which he had founded there.

The speed of Stephen's success had left Matilda far behind. She had made a miscalculation at the very start by making for Normandy rather than England when she heard the news of her father's death. It was a natural mistake for somebody of her continental background and ties, but a serious one. By the time she realised it, it was too late. Her behaviour may have been affected by the fact that she was pregnant, for many women feel sick and ill during the first weeks of pregnancy, and Matilda may simply not have felt up to the effort involved in making a winter crossing to England, with the possibility of a campaign to fight at the end of it.

She seems, in any case, to have had no suspicion that Stephen might try to claim the throne. Why should she? Twice over he had been amongst the first to make a vow to recognise her as heir and he had shown no trace of ambition to become king in the past. Whether they had been lovers or not, they had certainly been on terms of close friendship at Henry's court, and the news that he had usurped her throne must have been bitter indeed; perhaps, for the moment, shattering.

Worse news still was to come: Stephen had been recognised by the Pope. Matilda naturally sent envoys to Rome to plead her cause, and it is possible that the matter was considered at a council held at Pisa early in 1136. There is some evidence, however, for believing that her case may not have been argued before the Pope until 1139, but it is not decisive, and the earlier date does seem the more plausible. It would be difficult to account for a delay of three years before Matilda brought her case before the Papal court to protest at Stephen's perjury.

Whatever the date, the main events of the Council are not in dispute for they were recorded by John of Salisbury, who was there. Ulger, Bishop of Angers, was the chief spokesman for Matilda and he rested her case chiefly on the legitimacy of her claim to the throne as Henry's daughter and heir, on Stephen's broken oath and on his unjust seizure of the kingdom. Stephen's chief representative was Arnulf, Archdeacon of Séez and later Bishop of Lisieux, who made a stirring speech to the effect that Matilda, because of her unlawful birth, could not be regarded as Henry's rightful heir. Her mother, he said, had been a nun, 'dragged from her cloister, her veil torn from her'. As to Stephen's vow and the accusation of perjury, he alleged that the oath had been extorted from him, virtually by force, and in any case had been conditional on the King not changing his mind. But he *had* changed his mind; he had changed it on his deathbed and had declared Stephen his heir. This fact had been proved before the English Church and the Archbishop of Canterbury by the solemn oath of Hugh Bigod, supported by two knights. Stephen had been recognised as king by the bishops and all the leading men of the kingdom and his accession was now an established fact. Moreover, he had been crowned and anointed, and a matter of such great import could not be set on one side.

Bishop Ulger, who had a high reputation both for scholarship and character, then made a spirited reply on Matilda's behalf.

'I am astounded,' he said, 'at Arnulf's ingratitude and lack of scruple in attacking the late King, who was responsible for raising him, and all his family, from the dung. I am equally astonished at the sheer effrontery of his lies. But then his whole race is notorious for always being ready to say anything that suits their purpose. If they have any claim to distinction at all, it is for their depravity and utter shamelessness. When you attack the King, who is dead,' he said, turning to Arnulf, 'your lord whom you worshipped as long as he was alive, you are attacking the Church, for it was the Church which confirmed his marriage to the mother of Empress Matilda.' There had been nothing secret about that marriage; it was all open and above board. As for the claim that the King had changed his mind about the succession, this was proved to be false by the testimony of the men who were with him when he died. It was not possible for Arnulf or Earl Hugh to speak with any authority about the last wishes of the King.

'You were not there – not one of you!' he declared.

Gilbert Foliot, Abbot of Gloucester, who was also present at the Council, gives a slightly different account of what happened. According to him, the chief argument of Stephen's supporters was that if Henry I's marriage was not legal, then Matilda was not his rightful heir, and the oath sworn to recognise her automatically fell to the ground. He does not give Bishop Ulger's reply – he says in fact that none was made – but goes on to argue on his own account that it was sufficient that Anselm had fully investigated the allegation that Henry's Queen had been a nun, and had been satisfied that she was not. Anselm himself had officiated at the marriage – Anselm, who would have preferred to have had his hands cut off rather than stretch them out in wrong-doing.

When Ulger had finished his speech, Pope Innocent declined to hear any further argument, and, acting against the advice of his cardinals, he confirmed Stephen as King of England, at the same time accepting the very handsome gifts which Stephen had brought him.

'Peter has left home, and his house is given over to money-changers!' exclaimed Ulger in disgust.

One of the cardinals who had been particularly opposed to the Pope's decision later became Pope himself, and it was he who instructed the Archbishop of Canterbury not to allow any 'innovations' to be made in respect of the succession to the English crown. He thought Stephen's behaviour in seizing it had been rightly condemned and that the whole affair should be regarded as still in dispute. It was this, in later years, which stood in the way of Stephen's ambition to have his son Eustace crowned in his own lifetime.

In the meantime, however, Stephen's position had been endorsed by the Pope and he had a letter to prove it. It was, perhaps, less forthright than he might have wished. The Pope merely said that he was aware that Stephen had been chosen King by the unanimous wish and consent both of the magnates of the realm and of the people at large, and that he had been consecrated and crowned. The Pope recognised this fact, and also the fact that Stephen had promised obedience and reverence to the Church. He was also aware, he said, of his close relationship to the late King. In view of all this, he was 'pleased' at what had been done and received Stephen with paternal affection as a son of Holy Church. The whole letter adds up not so much to a confirmation of Stephen as King as a recognition, for diplomatic purposes, of something that was already an accomplished fact. None the less, it was of the greatest importance to Stephen, for if the Pope was prepared to countenance him, accusations of perjury, coming from other sources, were going to fall rather flat. He had acquired respectability from the Pope, if nothing else.

Matilda, in the meantime, had had a limited success in Normandy and one or two strong points, such as Domfront and Argentan, had been yielded up to her; but the picture changed as soon as her husband Geoffrey joined her with his Angevin troops. There was always hostility between the Normans and the Angevins, and on this occasion the Angevins do seem to have behaved with unusual savagery. The Normans were scarcely better, and after some bitter encounters, Geoffrey and Matilda retreated to their own country.

Stephen had failed to make an appearance, and his brother Theobald eventually agreed to a truce with the Angevins. The country then remained in a state of general unrest until September 1136, when another assault was launched by Geoffrey on his wife's behalf. Matilda did not accompany him this time as their third son, William, had been born on 21 July not much more than a month before. As soon as she was well enough, however, she raised a large army, probably numbering several thousands, and set off to join her husband.

She was too late. Geoffrey had had some successes initially, but there had been a setback before Lisieux as the inhabitants had chosen to burn their city to the ground rather than allow the

Angevins to enter it. The Angevins, overwhelmed by the heat of the flames, had decided that it was impossible to get near enough to the citadel to take it, and had turned aside to a village called Sap after a tall pine tree which stood near the church. An assault was launched, but the inhabitants put up a vigorous defence and during the fighting Geoffrey was severely wounded in the foot.

On that same day, 1 October, Matilda joined him but he was in pain from his wound and in no mood to make further efforts. He had had enough, he was going home. What was said between them is not known, but it is not difficult to imagine Matilda's frustration. She had borne a child two months before, she had risen from her bed and had immediately set about raising an army. She had left her baby son behind and had marched at the head of her men into Normandy to bring aid to her husband – who told her she could march them back again in the morning. A lot has been said of Matilda's 'arrogance', but she was clearly no match for her husband, for on the following morning the Angevins were seen to be in full retreat.

'The count, who had ridden into Normandy on a foam-flecked warhorse, uttering dire threats of vengeance,' wrote the Chronicler Orderic Vitalis, 'was brought home pale and groaning and carried in a litter.' He left behind him an even greater hatred of the Angevins than had existed before, for his men had burnt and looted, they had desecrated churches and stolen their sacred treasures, they had murdered and raped. And they had even managed to shock the Normans by their table manners, for they had 'eaten flesh either raw, or only half-cooked, and without either salt or bread'.

The winter, spent in inactivity at Angers, must have been a time of bitterness for Matilda. She had lost England, and, for the time being at least, it looked as though she had lost Normandy as well. She helped to nurse her husband's wound, and it may be that they developed some degree of solidarity in making plans for a new campaign in the spring; but it cannot have been easy to forget present failure.

For Stephen, on the other hand, everything seemed to be going well. After attending his uncle's funeral at Reading, he went on to Oxford, where he made a number of promises to the Church: he would not retain vacant sees in his possession and he would allow free canonical election. He would relax the harshness of the forest laws and he would abolish Danegeld, a tax originally imposed to provide resources to fight invasions by the Danes, and later continued as a land tax. Meanwhile, Matilda's uncle David, King of Scotland, the one leading magnate who seemed to interpret his oath to support Matilda as a solemn obligation, marched over the border and captured Newcastle. Stephen raised the 'largest army ever known within the memory of man', perhaps as many as ten thousand men; but he could afford it with his uncle's treasure at his back. He hurried north and met the Scottish king near Durham early in February, where he managed to pacify him with the promise of some rights in the earldom of Northumbria and the gift of a large part of Cumberland and Westmorland, a gift which he made not at his own expense, but at the expense of Ranulf, Earl of Chester, who had some claim to Carlisle. He also agreed that the earldom of Huntingdon should be held by King David's son Henry, who did homage to him for it. He then returned happily to London, taking Prince Henry with him, pleased that all had been settled so amicably; but the fact remained that King David himself had still refused to pay Stephen homage out of regard for his oath to his niece, and that the powerful Earl Ranulf was now a potential enemy.

Stephen held his Easter court in London, and it turned out to be a very different affair from his Christmas court. That had been a meagre gathering attended by only three bishops and very few of the leading nobles, but at Easter the court was crowded with the great men of the land, brilliant in their jewels, their furs and their fine robes; and on Easter day, Stephen's wife Matilda was crowned Queen in Westminster Abbey.

Stephen was established; but he made a mistake if he felt himself secure. He had honoured men whose support was important to him, but he had offended others, and it would not take a great deal to make him lose the friendship of those men who now seemed to be on his side. Even at this court, the Archbishop of Canterbury went off in a huff because Prince Henry of Scotland had been given his rightful place at the King's right hand. Moreover, Stephen had still received no recognition from Matilda's half-brother, Robert, Earl of Gloucester, one of the richest and most powerful men in the kingdom and the late King's natural son.

Robert of Gloucester was an outstanding man in every way – loyal, honest, intelligent and brave. William of Malmesbury, admittedly not an impartial witness since he was a protégé of Earl Robert, said that if any man was 'truly noble', it was he. It is not certain who his mother may have been, although it seems likely that she was the daughter of Robert Corbet of Caen; or she may just possibly have been the celebrated Princess Nesta of Wales, the Helen of Troy of her time. Nesta was certainly Henry I's mistress, and after a highly adventurous career she achieved lasting fame as the grandmother of the historian Giraldus Cambrensis.

Robert did not attend Stephen's Easter court because he was in something of a dilemma. He, like the other barons, had sworn a solemn oath to support his sister's claim to the throne, and, unlike most of the others, he felt a genuine scruple about breaking it. In any case, later events showed that his concern for Matilda was entirely genuine. On the other hand, her cause seemed for the moment to be lost, and if Robert came out in her favour, it would do her no good, but it would certainly do him harm. There was no immediate hope of opposing Stephen with success, for with Henry's vast treasure he could not only lavish gifts in all directions, but he could afford to employ a large army of mercenaries. If Robert wanted to help his sister, the most he could do was to try to win support for her when and where he could, while outwardly acquiescing in Stephen's rule.

He had so far ignored Stephen's messages and constantly repeated demands that he should come to him, but at last, in April 1136, he crossed from Normandy to England and paid formal homage to the King. The homage, however, was conditional. According to William of Malmesbury, he swore fealty only so long as Stephen maintained him in his present rank and fulfilled all his undertakings to him. None the less, the fact that he had received homage from Robert seemed to give the final touch to Stephen's triumph.

Robert stayed in Stephen's company for some time. He was still with him when the King went to Oxford after Easter and he witnessed a charter for him there. The Church, it seemed, had not been entirely satisfied by the undertakings given by Stephen a month or two before, and a certain amount of grumbling by the prelates had cast a slight shadow over his otherwise glittering Easter court. In Oxford, accordingly, he confirmed once more that the Church should be 'free'. Simony, the sale of ecclesiastical preferment, was to be forbidden and all the possessions and privileges of the Church were to be maintained exactly as they had been at the death of his grandfather, the Conqueror. Jurisdiction over men in holy orders was to remain in the hands of the bishops and Stephen promised not to interfere with the disposition of Church property when a death occurred. He promised to stamp out all injustices and exactions wherever they appeared, and he pledged himself to keep peace and do justice to all. He would give up the new forests acquired by his predecessor King Henry, and he undertook that when sees fell vacant, he would not keep them in his own hands. In general, he would observe the good laws and ancient customs of the land. The Church was satisfied with these concessions, and Stephen felt he could now look to it for support, an important matter for a king with a shaky title.

With few exceptions the most dangerous of his potential enemies had by this time recognised Stephen. He was on apparently friendly terms with King David of Scotland; Brian fitzCount, an old friend of Empress Matilda, had attended his Easter court and so had Miles of Gloucester, one of Henry I's Constables. Best of all, Robert of Gloucester was, so it seemed, prepared to establish good relations with him too. Perhaps the time had come when he could relax; he might well have thought so.

In fact, he was at the beginning of the long series of troubles which never entirely subsided during the whole of his turbulent reign. At the end of April, Stephen fell ill, a false report spread abroad that he was dead, and at once a number of minor revolts broke out. Hugh Bigod, perhaps feeling he had been insufficiently rewarded for the major service he had done the King by producing his story of King Henry's deathbed change of mind, proceeded to reward himself by taking possession of the castle of Norwich. Stephen promptly marched against him, forced him to surrender it without much difficulty, and pardoned him. Robert of Bampton, an Oxfordshire baron, then began to wage a private war on the surrounding countryside, but Stephen captured his castle, again without much trouble. There was disaffection of a far more serious kind to be faced, however.

One man of importance who had *not* attended Stephen's Easter court was Baldwin de Redvers, a man of high rank who had been on close terms with the late King. He seized the royal castle of Exeter and stocked it with provisions as though preparing for a siege. His armed bands of followers then began to throng the streets of Exeter, and their aspect was so menacing that the citizens sent off a message to Stephen asking him for help. Stephen, always prompt to take action, sent off an advance force of two hundred cavalry which managed to secure possession of the city, although they failed to take the castle. Soon afterwards, the King himself arrived with his army, and settled down to the long process of capture by siege.

It was not going to be an easy task to capture it, for it stood on a high mound, it was well fortified and had towers of 'hewn stone'. Stephen's force, however, was considerable and he probably welcomed the opportunity of displaying the fact that the barons who had attended his Easter court and had paid him homage were willing to do battle for him as well. To fight for your lord was, after all, one of the main duties of a vassal. But how well and how faithfully these men were prepared to fight was quite another matter. For instance, it was outwardly a triumph for Stephen that Robert of Gloucester was present with his army, but Stephen

would have lacked imagination if he had not occasionally
wondered whether he was an asset or a liability.

Baldwin's wife and sons were in the castle, but it is likely that
he was not there himself. The castle garrison, however, seemed
in good heart and enthusiastically shouted insults at the King's
army from the battlements. They followed this up with a rain of
arrows and an occasional sortie; but the King pressed his attack
with vigour and seems to have gained possession of the outer
wall of the castle and to have destroyed a bridge which connected
the castle to the town. Stephen himself took an active part in the
fighting and he engaged miners to undermine the fortifications.
Then one of Baldwin's supporters, Judhael of Totnes, together
with a band of his retainers, managed to mingle with Stephen's
army, and after smuggling a message through to the castle
garrison, they got themselves rushed inside under cover of a
sortie.

The fact that alien troops had been able to mix with the King's
army without being detected, and then join up with the enemy in
broad daylight, naturally caused both anger and embarrassment.
The rather thin excuse was put forward that the intruders had
been wearing armour, and in armour one man looked very like
another, but nobody believed that this coup could have been
brought off without at any rate some help from Stephen's
nominal supporters. Stephen himself decided to make the best
of the affair, observing that all would, under Providence, turn
out well in the end, and that the more of these malefactors who
were shut up in the castle, the better.

After three months of effort, it looked as though the siege was
going to be successful, for the castle began to run short of water,
always the point of danger for even the strongest fortress. There
was a severe drought that summer, the springs in the castle,
normally plentiful, began to dry up, and soon there was scarcely
any water at all. Wine, which was apparently in better supply,
had to be used for everything, for making bread, for cooking,
washing, and even for extinguishing the firebrands which
Stephen's engineers tossed over the castle walls. Thirst was first

of all a serious menace, then an anguish. And when the wine at last gave out as well, desperate consultations were held in the castle as to what should be done – what could be done. In fact, of course, there was nothing for it but surrender on the best terms obtainable.

Two envoys were sent to treat with Stephen, and Henry of Winchester, who was with him, at once noticed their distressed condition: their sagging skin and 'wasted appearance', their 'air of apathy', their dry lips and laboured breathing. And he realised that they were in an agony of thirst. From this he concluded that there was no need to discuss terms since they would be forced to surrender very soon in any case, and he persuaded the King to send them away without listening to them.

Next Baldwin's wife came to Stephen as a suppliant, with bare feet, ashes strewn on her head and weeping piteously. Stephen received her with courtesy, but Henry of Winchester again stiffened his resolution and she, too, was sent away. In the end, it was the barons of Stephen's own army who saved the garrison. Many of them were related by ties of blood to the besieged and they had no desire to see them die, or even decisively defeated. They were not, after all, particularly enthusiastic about Stephen, while they had interests in common with the men in the castle.

They went to the King and appealed to him for clemency. It was enough, surely, they said, for the castle to be surrendered to him. It would be more fitting to his dignity as a king and to his humanity as a man if he spared the lives of those whom he had forced to surrender. Let them go in peace, they begged him. After all, these were men who had never sworn homage to him personally, and they were but obeying the commands of their lord, as they must.

This was a strange argument to use for it suggested that the King had no claim on the loyalty of the people as a whole but only on those leading barons who had actually paid homage to him; but it prevailed. Stephen allowed the defenders of the castle to go away unharmed, and even to retain their arms. He would have done better to stand firm, as Henry of Winchester kept urging, for such extreme good nature was interpreted as a sign of weakness; it was also a demonstration of the fact that his army could not be depended upon to back him beyond a certain point. But the whole episode was typical of Stephen's character and behaviour. He was prompt in action, he fought well, and then somehow or other, through excessive good nature or lack of resolution, he would lose his advantage and the whole affair would peter out with nothing much achieved.

Baldwin was not moved to gratitude by the King's generosity. On the contrary, he hurried off to the Isle of Wight, which formed part of his lands, and established himself in his castle there, meaning to plunder the ships which plied between Normandy and England carrying supplies. There were limits to Stephen's tolerance, however, and he began assembling a fleet at Southampton to invade the island. Baldwin did not stay to fight. He knew that his castle had only limited supplies of water, so he made formal submission to the King and went off into exile. In fact, he joined Matilda and Geoffrey in Anjou, who were naturally delighted to receive him, especially as he was determined to stir up all the trouble he could against the King. He complained to his friends that he had been persecuted by Stephen and begged them to help him. Urged on by Empress Matilda, he also made sudden forays into Normandy, and in general became an energetic supporter of her claim to the English throne.

In England, however, Stephen once more seemed secure, and he began to make preparations to cross the Channel and meet the challenge facing him in Normandy. Before doing so, however, he went hunting at Brampton, near Huntingdon, and there he held a forest assize at which he enforced the old forest laws which he had made a solemn oath to abandon or relax.

At Exeter, he had demonstrated an ill-judged weakness in letting rebels go free, and now he had demonstrated a lack of good faith in breaking a promise which should have been binding. 'He was a mild man, soft and good, and did no justice,' said a contemporary; it seems a fair summary of his character.

4 Turbulence and Disaffection ⁊

Castle life in winter must have been trying at the best of times what with the cold, the damp and the ceaseless draughts. The windows were scarcely more than slits so that the light indoors was poor, and in the evenings there were only candles to see by, or peeled rushes soaked in fat. The food tended to be monotonous as few animals could be kept during the winter owing to the scarcity of winter feed. They were generally slaughtered in the autumn and the flesh salted down – not always successfully – to preserve it. In fact the frequency with which food had to be eaten which was more or less tainted was one of the reasons for the lavish use of spices in the Middle Ages. Wine, however, was plentiful, and beer and mead were drunk as well.

Matilda was accustomed, of course, to the physical discomforts of her time and Angers castle was better than most. By the standards of the day, in fact, it was luxurious; but as the slow winter wore on, it is unlikely that either its comforts, or its splendid outlook over the great curve of the river Maine, provided Matilda with much consolation for her lost glories as Empress, and for the more immediate loss of her prospects as heiress to the English throne. How did she pass the time? It is difficult to picture her settling down to tapestry or needlework, or spending domestic evenings playing backgammon with her husband. It is easier to imagine her pacing the battlements in a fury of frustration. Geoffrey's outlook must have seemed to her provincial and mediocre, for, as an Angevin, he thought only of extending his power over Normandy, and even there he tried to keep his wife, the true heir to the Duchy, in the background.

With the spring of 1137, however, there was a return of activity on both sides. Fifteen months had passed since Stephen's accession to the throne, and at last he was ready to make an expedition to Normandy to claim his rights there. He landed at La Hougue in March 1137 and found the Duchy in a very disordered state, exposed to raids by the Angevins and with practically every baron making his own bid for independence and power. Stephen's first act was to make a settlement with his brother Theobald of Blois, who had shown such generosity in withdrawing his own claim to the English throne and in making at least some attempt to look after Stephen's interests in Normandy. Stephen met him at Evreux and promised to pay him a pension of two thousand marks of silver a year. It was a handsome sum, but not over-generous in the circumstances. Stephen, with his spendthrift ways, was already becoming conscious that the vast treasure he had acquired from his uncle Henry I was not limitless, and that a good deal of it was already gone.

In May, he had a meeting with Louis VI of France and paid homage to him as Duke of Normandy. They made a treaty of friendship which may not have meant very much in itself, but was important to Stephen in that the French King thereby gave him formal recognition as Duke.

His next task was to deal with Geoffrey of Anjou, who had launched a new assault on Normandy in May. Geoffrey had again alienated the Normans by the brutality of his tactics – 'fire, pillage and slaughter' – but he had none the less advanced to within ten miles of Caen which was in the custody of Robert of Gloucester. No doubt he hoped that Robert, who had crossed over to Normandy on Easter Day, would join him. The garrison at Caen remained faithful to Stephen, however, and in June Stephen collected an army at Lisieux with the intention of driving Geoffrey back into Anjou.

Stephen's army, unfortunately for him, turned out to be no more reliable than the army with which he had besieged Exeter castle, but for different reasons. He had become very friendly with William of Ypres, a natural son of Philip, Count of Ypres, who had lived a life of adventure and violence, and was probably implicated in the murder of Charles the Good, Count of Flanders, whose inheritance he had claimed. He had previously been employed as an agent by Henry I in various intrigues, and when he was driven out of Flanders, he had fled to England. There he had attached himself to Stephen, and when Stephen successfully claimed the crown, he made William the commander of his army of mercenaries.

William of Ypres and his Flemings had already made themselves unpopular in England. A large influx of foreigners is likely to be unwelcome at any time, but at least under Henry I they had generally arrived in pursuit of trade and were a source of profit. Under Stephen, the Flemings had come over as soldiers and had created violence and disorder wherever they went. In Normandy, where they formed part of Stephen's army, they became a focus of discontent among the other barons, and William himself was responsible for giving Stephen a piece of thoroughly bad advice.

William either genuinely suspected Robert of Gloucester of treachery, or else he was jealous of his power and his potential influence over Stephen. At all events, he persuaded Stephen to lay an ambush for him. The plan was betrayed, however, and Robert escaped unharmed. After that, he naturally kept well away from the King, in spite of repeated invitations to come and join him. Stephen realised that Robert must have learnt of his treachery, and when at last they did meet, he seems to have tried to pass the whole thing off with vague phrases of goodwill. Never again would he do such a terrible thing, he said. He even swore an oath, in the presence of the Archbishop of Rouen, that his friendship for Robert in the future would be unfailing and true. But it takes more than bland and smiling assurances to wipe out an attempted ambush, and Robert felt no confidence at all in his promises. He was right not to do so, for although Stephen continued to be ostentatiously friendly when he was there, he abused him wholeheartedly when he was not. Robert gave no sign that he was aware of this, however, and he stayed on in Normandy for the rest of the year, brooding uncomfortably on his broken oath to his sister, and waiting for an opportunity to give her his support openly.

William did not lose Stephen's favour as a result of alienating Robert of Gloucester; on the contrary, he seemed more in his favour than ever, a fact which began to annoy the Norman barons. It annoyed them so much, in fact, that they refused to fight under William's command and quarrelling broke out between their men and the Flemings. The quarrels eventually became so violent that a number of men were killed and the Normans made off home in disgust without even taking leave of the King, much less asking his permission. In feudal terms, this was not far from an act of open rebellion.

Stephen's army crumbled away, his plans were in ruins and by the end of June he was happy to conclude a truce with Geoffrey by which he agreed to pay him two thousand marks of silver a year. Geoffrey prudently demanded – and obtained – the first year's payment in advance.

Peace of a sort was thus restored to Normandy, and Stephen decided to go back to England, which was by this time anything but peaceful. Before leaving Normandy, however, he appointed two deputies, William de Roumare and Roger of the Cotentin, to try to keep order in the Duchy while he was away.

In England, Stephen had to face outbreaks of disaffection on every hand, for the whole of his fragile network of good relations with the English barons seemed to be breaking up. They began asking for favours in return for continued loyalty – castles, lands, titles. He gave what they asked, he allowed them to fortify their castles, he was lavish with what remained of King Henry's treasure; but he did not win their loyalty. And because of his army of Flemish mercenaries – 'savage and rapacious' – together with an ever-increasing influx of foreigners, his popularity with the people at large was also diminishing fast. It was particularly resented that the notorious William of Ypres was now his chief adviser.

Rebellion was breaking out in so many different places at once that it was difficult for Stephen to know where to go first. On

Christmas Eve he hurried to Bedford and laid siege to the castle there, but he had hardly secured it before he heard news of trouble in the north. King David of Scotland had demanded the earldom of Northumberland for his son, saying it had been promised to him the year before, and when it was refused, he led an army over the border. His soldiers behaved with revolting savagery. They 'ripped open pregnant women, tossed children on their spears, slaughtered priests and desecrated churches'. It amused them to cut off the heads of sacred images and substitute the heads of their murdered victims. Stephen hurried north in February 1138 to deal with this invasion, but after some indecisive skirmishing, he was forced to retire through lack of provisions, and the Scots immediately resumed their destruction and pillaging throughout Northumberland.

King David himself had not been implicated in these outrages, but he was, of course, responsible for the invasion, and he may very well have been influenced by the letters he was receiving from Matilda. He was her uncle, he was one of the very few who had refused to do homage to Stephen out of respect for the oath he had sworn to recognise Matilda, and she must have felt him to be an important ally from the beginning. She wrote constantly to him to plead for support, pointing out that she had been deprived of all she might have expected under her father's will, and that she had been robbed of the crown promised to her by the solemn oath of the clerics and nobles of England. The law had been set aside, she said, and justice trodden underfoot.

Matilda also sent him messages by her friends in the north, chief among them Eustace fitzJohn, lord of the castles of Bamburgh and Alnwick, who had been a friend of her father King Henry. David entertained him and other supporters of the Angevin cause at his court, and by May fitzJohn had openly declared his support for Matilda. Stephen, however, was almost too preoccupied with the grave news he was receiving from Normandy to react at once to this new threat in the north, for Matilda had not contented herself with writing letters to King David, but had been actively seeking help in every direction she could. She and Geoffrey had managed to establish contact with Robert of Gloucester, who had no reason to feel any affection for Stephen after the affair of the ambush, and they had been discussing plans together. They had agreed that the time had not yet come for an invasion of England, and Geoffrey of Anjou had in any case never shown much enthusiasm for such a project. Normandy was, for him, the obvious target, and in June he once more launched an attack there, so breaking his truce with Stephen. With Robert's connivance, several towns of importance, including Bayeux and Caen, submitted to him.

Robert of Gloucester, following the strict forms of feudal etiquette, now sent a formal 'defiance' to Stephen; that is, he gave him notice that he no longer recognised him as his overlord and would no longer carry out his feudal obligations to him. He did not himself go over to England immediately, but his 'defiance' was the signal for revolt to blaze out, first in one place, then in another, but particularly in Robert's own lands in the south and west. Other barons, such as William fitz John of Harptree near Bristol, Ralph Lovell at Castle Cary and William de Mohun of Ludlow castle began to join him in opposition to Stephen, until, beset by dangers on every side, Stephen went off to London to confer with his advisers there. He decided to send two of his most trusted friends, Waleran of Meulan and William of Ypres, to Normandy to see what they could do to restore the situation there, while he himself went to the West Country, the centre of Robert's power and influence.

The capture of Bristol was obviously of the first importance, but Stephen had made the mistake of allowing Robert's messengers to travel on there after delivering his 'defiance' to the King, and they had carried with them instructions from Robert to provision the garrison and take all measures possible to harass the King's adherents. Stephen must surely have guessed that this was what they were likely to do, and allowing them to go free was another instance of his disastrous 'mildness'. Henry I might have hanged them; at the least, he would have kept them under his control.

Bristol castle was a handsome stone building and well situated

from the point of view of defence for it had water on three sides
while the fourth rose sheer from the ground. Robert himself had
strengthened the fortifications and its capture was bound to be a
major enterprise. Every hour of delay enabled the defenders to
increase their stock of provisions and make ready for resistance,
but Stephen, unusually for him, seemed in no great hurry to
begin the siege. It was nearly the end of June before he reached
Bristol with his army, and when he did arrive, he seemed curiously
disheartened from the start by the prospect facing him. The siege
of a strong and well-equipped castle could be long, trying and
tedious, but given enough men to make certain that no reinforce-
ments or provisions arrived, the end could only be a question of
time. Sooner or later, the food, if not the water, was bound to
run out. Bristol castle was likely to hold out longer than most
since it had access to the sea and a good port, but it could have
been reduced in the end.

Stephen consulted his barons as to what he should do, and as
usual his army let him down. One party was for energetic action:
they advised him to block one approach to the city by building a
dam below it where the river was narrowest. They could fill in the
channel, they said, with a huge pile of rocks, timber and earth,
and so make it impossible for any ship to reach the port. Forts
should also be built on each side of the city to prevent the use of
the bridges. The King and his army, encamped before the castle,
could then wait for famine and distress to bring about the surrender of the garrison.

Another party, however, possibly traitorous, ridiculed these
suggestions, saying it was absurd to think of blocking up such a
mighty river with rocks or timber or anything else. The obstruction
would only sink in the mud or be swept out to sea. Far better,
they told him, to give up the idea of taking Bristol and turn his
energies to capturing prizes that would be more easily obtained
and more immediately profitable.

Unfortunately for Stephen, he listened to the latter advice and
turned away from Bristol, so leaving it to become one of the
main headquarters of Matilda's party for the rest of the war.

Only pausing to lay waste the area immediately surrounding Bristol, he marched off with his army in pursuit of easier prey. He went first to Castle Cary and starved it into surrender without much difficulty. After that, he took the castle at Harptree by storm, and then looked round for fresh successes.

Wherever he looked there was trouble – he could have marched in almost any direction and found rebels to subdue. He chose to march north into Shropshire where William fitzAlan, the castellan of Shrewsbury castle, had declared for Earl Robert and was preparing for resistance. When he heard the news of the King's approach, however, he fled with his wife and children, leaving his uncle Ernulf behind. Ernulf put up a spirited resistance, but the castle fell in the end and he was captured. This time Stephen was determined not to repeat his past mistake of being over-lenient, for he had begun to realise that his barons despised him for it, so he hanged Ernulf and executed ninety-three of his followers as well.

His sternness seemed, in the short term, to have an excellent effect, for a number of Ernulf's supporters in the district came to offer their services to Stephen and hand over the keys of their fortresses. There was good news, too, from Stephen's Queen, who had just succeeded in capturing Dover castle.

These minor successes were overshadowed, however, by the increasing gravity of the news from the north, where King David of Scotland was once more active. At the end of July 1138, he had crossed the border and invaded Yorkshire, but Stephen was too occupied in putting down rebellions in the south to go to the help of the Yorkshiremen. As it turned out, he was not needed. Fired with a passionate determination to defend their land and their homes, the men of Yorkshire, with the old and sick Archbishop Thurstan of York at their head, made ready to do battle with the Scots. First of all, Thurstan assembled the barons, and reminding them that their cause was just, since they were defending their fatherland, he said that every parish priest would lead his flock to the battle. He himself would be at the head of the army, even though he was so frail and ill that he would have to be

c

carried in a litter. But no, they told him, it was his prayers that they wanted. He must wrestle for them in prayer in his own cathedral church while they went forth to battle.

The leaders drew up their men in battle array at Cowton Moor near Northallerton, vowing that they would keep faith with each other, and that they would be victorious or die. In their midst, as a rallying point, they had erected their 'Standard', which consisted of a ship's mast fixed to a cart. At the top of the mast was a silver pyx containing the Host, and the mast itself was hung with the banners of three local churches, St Peter of York, St John of Beverley, and St Wilfred of Ripon.

Walter Espec, the sheriff of Yorkshire, took his stand on the cart and gave an eve of battle address to the army, while the Bishop of Durham, who represented the sick Archbishop, pronounced absolution on all those who might die that day. And so, in a spirit of sacrifice and dedication, the men of Yorkshire made ready for battle.

David of Scotland had far less tractable material to work with. He had wanted to draw up his troops in formal battle array, but the men of Galloway, half-savage and quite beyond his control, shouted at him that they would go further with their bare breasts than any of his knights tricked out in fancy armour. They would form the vanguard, they said; and King David, fearing an outbreak of violence if he attempted to thwart them, let them have their way.

The battle began in the morning of 22 August 1138 and the half-naked men of Galloway duly charged to cries of 'Alban! Alban!', their country's war cry. But their spears and javelins glanced uselessly off the enemy's shields, while the arrows of the English 'buzzed like bees and flew like rain', piercing their bare chests. It was not what they had expected, and they turned and ran. Their flight threw into confusion the knights who were coming up behind them and the panic spread. Prince Henry of Scotland had some success with an attack against the Yorkshiremen's flank, but it could not change the course of the battle. Soon the Scottish army was in full retreat and King David was left almost alone, desperately attempting to rally his supporters. But it was hopeless. His friends, fearing that he would be captured, at last persuaded him to jump on a horse and escape while he could.

The carnage was dreadful. According to one report, eleven thousand Scots lay dead on the field of battle, but this figure must be an exaggeration. Very many men died, however, and many more were later captured and slain. King David had to ride seventy miles, all the way to Carlisle, before he felt it safe to rest, and it was three days before his son Henry managed to join him there.

For Matilda waiting in Anjou, the news of her uncle's defeat must have been devastating; but it had been an unhappy summer for her altogether. It had begun well with Robert of Gloucester's desertion of Stephen, the news of widespread revolts in England and Geoffrey's minor successes in Normandy, but these advantages had not been followed up. Robert ought to have gone at once to England to defend his lands there and rally support for the Empress, but he had delayed and had then found that the chief ports on the south coast had fallen into Stephen's hands, making a successful landing almost impossible. In Normandy, Geoffrey had failed to follow up his first successes; far from it. Hearing that Stephen's generals, Waleran of Meulan and William of Ypres, were assembling a large army to march against him, he had made a precipitate retreat, leaving Earl Robert to hold out on his own in Caen.

On balance, Matilda was scarcely nearer being able to claim her inheritance in either Normandy or England than she had been at the beginning of the year, for although her rival Stephen had had his reverses, at least he was still on the throne, while the most powerful of her own supporters, King David of Scotland, had been so decisively defeated that it would be a long time before she could look to him for help again. In fact he concluded a peace with Stephen in April of the following year.

As the winter of 1138 set in, the future must have seemed bleak to Matilda. Stephen, however, had already made a mistake which was to have the effect of seriously undermining his position as King.

5 An Encounter with Bishops

William of Corbeil, Archbishop of Canterbury, died in November 1136, not long after he had crowned Stephen King, a just punishment, according to the Chronicler Henry of Huntingdon, for having broken his vow to recognise Matilda as heir to the throne. The obvious candidate to succeed him was the King's brother, Henry of Winchester. In fact, his election seemed so much a foregone conclusion that Henry made an approach to the Pope to find out whether there would be any difficulty about his translation from one see to the other.

Henry was not only the obvious candidate, he was a very suitable one as well. He was an exceptionably able man and although some people might have preferred an Archbishop of a more spiritual cast of mind, there was very little otherwise that could be said against him. He was certainly guilty of 'plurality' in that he had retained the office of Abbot of Glastonbury after becoming Bishop of Winchester, but it was a common enough practice at the time and there were no darker scandals attached to his name. He spent lavishly on himself, but he was also generous in his gifts to the Church. If he built himself a splendid palace at Winchester, he also carried out extensive building at his Abbey of Glastonbury and in his own cathedral. He had also presented his cathedral with a number of magnificent gifts, including the great cross itself, glittering with over two hundred precious stones and containing relics, so it was said, of the True Cross, the Lord's manger and cradle, hair from the head of the Blessed Virgin, relics of Abraham, Isaac and an imposing list of saints, ending up with a fragment of the stone used by Jacob as a pillow. If he did not spend his nights wrestling in prayer or 'baring his back to the lash', he was outstanding in the more pedestrian acts of piety expected of a bishop. He gave alms on a huge scale, and in 1137 he founded the St Cross Hospital at Winchester for 'thirteen poor impotent men so reduced in strength as rarely or never to be able to raise themselves without the assistance of another'. These men were to have garments and beds suitable to their infirmities, 'good wheaten bread daily of the weight of five marks, and three dishes at dinner and one at supper suitable to the day, and drink of good quality'. This charity, incidentally, is carried on in modified form at the present day, and dry bread and a sup of ale is given free to anyone who claims it before supplies run out.

Apart from his personal suitability to be Archbishop of Canterbury, Henry had rendered a great service to his brother. It is quite possible that Stephen would never have become King without his brother's backing and it would be natural enough if Henry expected something in return. Yet the whole of 1137 passed and the greater part of the following year, and still the See of Canterbury lay vacant.

By the summer of 1138, the Pope began to lose patience with the situation; it looked as though Stephen, in spite of his promises, was going to turn out as bad as his predecessors in the matter of vacant sees. The Pope accordingly sent over Alberic, Bishop of Ostia, to act as Papal Legate in England, and he called a Council of bishops, abbots and other leading churchmen to deal with the matter.

According to strict canon law, the election of an archbishop of Canterbury lay in the hands of the monks of Canterbury, but in practice no king had failed to exercise considerable, if not decisive influence on elections in the past. On this occasion, however, Stephen does seem to have held himself aloof, perhaps because he did not want to become closely involved. He was only too conscious of the debt he owed his brother, and he knew his brother's wishes; but gratitude can become a burden after a time and Stephen may well have resented feeling perpetually under an obligation. Henry was normally a tactful man, but he may not always have been able to resist reminding Stephen of how much he owed him, and it would be understandable if Stephen, for his part, was not anxious for his brother, a man far more gifted than he was, to become Archbishop of Canterbury, particularly as the Archbishop had a traditional right to be the King's chief adviser and held a rank only a little below that of the King himself.

The Council was duly held at Westminster on 11 December 1138, and towards the end of it, on 24 December, Henry of Winchester was absent for a brief period as he had to carry out an ordination; and it was during his absence that a new Archbishop was hastily elected. He was *not* to be Henry of Winchester, but Theobald of Bec, a surprise candidate.

Henry was beside himself with rage and made no secret of the fact. It probably added an extra spark to his fury that Theobald was of no great standing in the Church and was relatively unknown. He was thought to be a man of 'admirable' character – rather lukewarm praise – and Gervase of Canterbury merely remarked that he had a 'simple nature' with only 'slight claim to learning'. He had acquitted himself reasonably well as Abbot of Bec, and the future was to show him capable of real generosity and courage, but at the time his choice must have seemed puzzling in the extreme; perhaps he was the only candidate on whom everybody could agree. The Abbey of Bec, of course, did shed distinction on him, for the great Archbishops Lanfranc and Anselm had been Abbots of Bec in their day. As against this, the Abbey was a particular favourite of Empress Matilda, which could hardly have recommended its Abbot to Stephen.

Whatever was at the back of the choice of Theobald as Archbishop, whatever the arguments that prevailed, there can be no argument at all about the fact that Stephen had created for himself a new enemy when he already had enemies enough. Henry was said to have broken off the ceremony of ordination on which he was engaged as soon as the news of Theobald's election reached him and to have gone off in disgust. There was certainly an underhand flavour to an election hustled through at the precise moment when Henry was not there. Stephen did give a sort of consolation prize to Henry by allowing him to accept the office of Papal Legate the following year, but it was a foolish gesture for it put Henry in a position to exact a very complete revenge when the opportunity came. It also placed Theobald in an anomalous situation, since he was head of the Church in England, yet subordinate to Henry as Papal Legate.

Stephen, in spite of his local successes against rebels, and in spite of the resounding victory won by the Yorkshiremen over David of Scotland, was finding his position ever more harassing as one outbreak of rebellion succeeded another. 'They have elected me king, so why do they desert me?' he kept complaining. 'By the birth of God, I will never be called a fallen king.' His strength at the beginning had been largely due to his possession of Henry I's treasure, but Stephen had spent lavishly on foreign mercenaries, and on bribes and gifts to win support, and money was running short. With expensive campaigns on his hands, he was driven to the expedient of debasing the coinage. Money was no longer 'honest money', for by the King's order the coin of the realm was considerably lighter in weight than it had been before.

Amid all the distress and worry of the time, Stephen turned increasingly towards new friends and advisers, and in particular to the twins Waleran of Meulan and the hunchbacked Robert of Leicester. They, like Stephen, had been brought up at Henry's court and had earned an early reputation for brilliance by disputing successfully with cardinals when they were only eleven. Waleran had later rebelled against Henry, but had managed to get back into favour, and he had been a favourite of Stephen's since the beginning of his reign. Stephen had given him lands and castles, he had put the two brothers in charge of Normandy and he had even betrothed his two-year-old daughter to Waleran. The twins were hated by Henry of Winchester, however, and they in turn were predictably jealous of what power remained to him. Moreover, Waleran of Meulan was connected with Bec – he was a lay patron – and Henry may have thought that he had some-

thing to do with the choice of Theobald of Bec as Archbishop of
Canterbury.

Waleran and his twin must at all events have been delighted
that Henry was not to be Archbishop and that any further rise in
his influence and importance seemed satisfactorily blocked. There
was still one man, however, whose practical influence in affairs
compared with their own: Henry 1's old Justiciar, Roger, Bishop
of Salisbury.

Hardworking, resourceful, utterly faithful, he had been
Henry 1's chief minister, and at first Stephen had seemed to
favour him as much as his uncle had. 'I would give him half my
kingdom, if he asked for it,' he used to say, 'until his time is past.
He will grow tired of asking before I grow tired of giving.' This
was taken as a mark of trust and affection, but it was a remark, of
course, which could have more than one meaning. It could have
been slightly barbed. At all events, Waleran of Meulan set about
warning the King that Roger of Salisbury was contemplating
treason. He had, he reminded Stephen, been deeply attached to the
late king and he had made a vow to recognise his daughter;
perhaps he now regretted that he had not kept it. The story was
put about that Roger was in correspondence with Empress
Matilda and that he was completely committed to the Angevin
cause. Waleran and his friends also pointed to what was un-
doubtedly a fact, that the Bishop possessed large and formidable
castles, all of which he had built or restored himself, such as
Sherborne, Malmesbury, Salisbury and, above all, Devizes. Why
should a churchman, they asked, need such strongholds, such
large and well-armed bands of retainers, and, most suspicious
of all, why was Roger stocking his castles with provisions and
arms? Surely it would be sensible to arrest him, together with his
son Roger le Poer, who was in the powerful position of Chancellor. And what about Roger's almost equally powerful and
wealthy nephews Bishop Alexander of Lincoln and Bishop Nigel
of Ely, the King's Treasurer? They need only be held, they
argued, until they yielded up their fortresses to the King, so
rendering unto Caesar those things which were Caesar's. As

churchmen, they could scarcely make objection to such a reasonable demand.

Stephen hesitated. It was true that a vast amount of power was concentrated in this one family, and that they did, in effect, control all the practical administration of the kingdom. Perhaps, he thought, they were indeed a danger. But to arrest them on mere suspicion, to arrest, in particular, churchmen, no matter how much it might be argued that they were arrested not in the capacity of bishops but as dissident vassals of the King, this could be extremely dangerous. It could bring disaster.

Whether Bishop Roger and his relatives were in fact contemplating treason, whether they were really in touch with Empress Matilda, will never be known. It is quite possible that they were merely indulging a desire for self-aggrandisement in building their imposing castles; or else, worried by the uncertainty of the times, they may have been taking what seemed to them sensible precautions to protect themselves. Whatever the true facts of the case, it seems certain that Waleran of Meulan put forward a plan to Stephen by which he could render them harmless once and for all. It was ingenious, but as it involved no less than the arrest of three bishops – three leading churchmen – with all the repercussions that this would involve in Stephen's relations with the Church, Stephen, understandably, continued to hesitate for some time; but in the end, he was unable to resist Waleran's persuasions, and the plot was set in train.

A Great Council, an assembly of all the leading nobles and churchmen of the land, was held at Oxford on 24 June 1139, and the three bishops, together with Roger of Salisbury's son the Chancellor, were naturally called on to attend. For some reason, Bishop Roger felt disinclined to go.

'By my Lady St Mary,' he said, 'I don't know why it is, but I feel reluctant to set out on this journey. There is one thing I do know and that is that I shall be as much use in this Council as a colt on the battlefield.'

On the face of it, this seems a strange remark to come from the most experienced statesman and administrator in the kingdom;

but it may, of course, have had a deeper meaning. He may have begun to have doubts of the King's good faith, or he may even have heard rumours of a plot against him. However, he had no choice but to attend, and the plot went forward as planned.

A quarrel about lodgings was engineered between Roger of Salisbury's men and the followers of Alan, Count of Brittany, and however artificial the quarrel had been at the beginning, there was nothing artificial about the violence with which it was conducted. Bishop Roger's men jumped up from the table where they had been having a meal, their swords drawn, and it soon became obvious amid the clash of steel, the shouts and the uproar, that serious fighting was taking place. Count Alan's nephew was seriously wounded, as well as a number of other men, and one knight was killed.

That was the preliminary. The Bishop of Salisbury himself knew nothing of what had been going on for he was sitting in his own room apart when soldiers suddenly burst in and commanded him to come into the King's presence and answer a charge of disturbing the King's peace.

The accounts of the incident up to this point do show some discrepancies, but of what happened next there seems to be no doubt at all. Roger of Salisbury was arrested, together with his son and Bishop Alexander of Lincoln. Bishop Nigel of Ely was staying in lodgings outside the town and heard the news of what had happened in time to make his escape.

The arrested men were called on to answer the charges brought against them, but in fact they could have brought a charge on their own account against the King. By the standards of the day, Stephen had committed a grave breach of trust in arresting men who had come to his court, since they were officially in 'the King's peace' and entitled to the King's protection.

Stephen declared that the only way the bishops could give him satisfaction was by surrendering the keys of their castles as proof of their loyalty. The Bishops demurred. They were reluctant to leave themselves defenceless, particularly in view of what had happened, and they tried to stave off giving their consent.

At this point, however, the news arrived that Bishop Nigel of Ely had escaped and it was too late. He had fled to Devizes castle, laying waste the land all round it on the way, and had made ready to stand a siege. Stephen took this as an admission of guilt on the part of the bishops and was suddenly transported with rage. Bishop Alexander of Lincoln was at once thrown into prison and William of Ypres was ordered off to Devizes in pursuit of Nigel of Ely.

The King himself followed, taking Roger of Salisbury and his son Roger le Poer with him. When they reached Devizes, he imprisoned them separately. Bishop Roger was insultingly confined in a dilapidated cowshed, while his son was held apart with a rope round his neck. Devizes castle was closely guarded against the King and it was clear that Bishop Nigel was determined to defend it to the last. The King had hostages, however, and he did not scruple to use them. He 'pinched' the Bishop of Salisbury with hunger, threatening to starve him to death, while his son was led out on to a gallows, the rope ready round his neck. The King said that he would be hanged before the castle gates, in full sight of the rebels, if the castle were not surrendered to him immediately.

Bishop Roger was convinced by now that surrender was the only means of saving his son's life, as well as his own, and he pleaded with Nigel of Ely to hand over the castle to the King. He was bitterly angry, in any case, that Nigel had chosen to take refuge in Devizes instead of in some castle of his own.

Nigel remained unmoved by the Bishop's pleadings; he had no intention of submitting to the King. He was not, however, in undisputed control of the castle, for Maud of Ramsbury, the Bishop's mistress of twenty years' standing and the mother of their son, was in the castle as well, and she was determined that her son should not die if she could prevent it.

'It was I that bore him,' she said. 'It is not for me to have any part in his death. It would be better for me to lay down my own life in exchange for his.'

She sent a message to the King offering him the castle as a

ransom for the lives of Bishop Roger and their son Roger le Poer, and the offer was accepted. Nigel of Ely was shamed into giving reluctant agreement and Roger of Salisbury, the great Justiciar, the wealthy and powerful bishop, was at last released from his cowshed and allowed to go free. But he was a broken man and he never recovered.

Stephen was exuberant, for he could seize all Bishop Roger's vast treasure. He was in funds again. He was able not only to fill up his treasury but still have enough money left over to arrange a marriage between his son Eustace and Constance, the sister of Louis of France; an arrangement calling for considerable expenditure.

Stephen was not content with seizing Bishop Roger's treasure and castles, for he turned next to his other prisoner, Bishop Alexander of Lincoln. Alexander was dragged to the gates of his favourite castle of Newark, an elaborate structure which was his pride and joy, and told that he would be starved to death unless he surrendered it to the King. He did surrender it. He was then made to hand over his castle at Sleaford as well. As for Nigel of Ely, he was declared a traitor, and was soon in open revolt against the King.

It was a heady few weeks for Stephen. He had thrown off his 'soft and mild' aspect, he had been ruthless and brutal, and how well it had paid him! Waleran, too, must have felt triumphant at the success of his scheme; but retribution was to come. A storm of disapproval and outrage broke over the King. Strictly speaking, he had been acting within his rights in demanding the surrender of the bishops' castles, for the crown had the right to take control of all castles on demand. Moreover, in this case Stephen felt that he had had good reason to suspect the bishops' loyalty; but it was his abuse of hospitality which stuck in the minds of his contemporaries, and far far worse even than that was the fact that he had laid violent hands on churchmen, the 'Lord's anointed'.

There was also a point of law to be considered. Churchmen claimed the right, if they had committed a misdemeanour, or even a grave crime, to be tried only in the Church courts where the penalties tended to be very light, even negligible. Stephen had specifically conceded this right in the charter which he had given to the Church at Oxford three years before, so he was on weak ground if he attempted to dispute it. If, therefore, the bishops had committed an offence, they should have been handed over to the Church courts. Instead of that, they had been imprisoned, degraded, and put in danger of their lives by a secular ruler. The Church had no intention whatsoever of tolerating such behaviour, and the mouthpiece of the Church on this occasion was the King's brother, Henry of Winchester, now no longer his whole-hearted supporter but a man whom he had bitterly offended. As Papal Legate, it was for him to take the lead if anything was to be done, and he proceeded to discuss the affair with Theobald, Archbishop of Canterbury. He then sent a summons to the King to appear before a Council of the Church which was to be held at Winchester on 29 August 1139.

The Council was well attended, almost the only absentees being Thurstan, Archbishop of York, who excused himself on the grounds of ill-health, and Alexander of Lincoln. Theobald of Canterbury was there, in spite of the fact that his position was mildly embarrassing since the Bishop of Winchester, his inferior in the hierarchy of the Church, was in charge of the proceedings as Papal Legate.

The Bishop opened the meeting by making an address in Latin. He began by sketching in the events which had taken place at the Council at Oxford and subsequently at Devizes. He said that the King, led astray by unscrupulous men, had committed a 'lamentable crime' in that he had ordered subjects, and worse still, bishops, to suffer violence while in the protection of his court. He had followed this up with another serious offence, an offence against God, in that he had seized church property. He himself, he said, had reproached the King for what he had done. Now it was for the Archbishop and the other ecclesiastics present to decide what action was appropriate; as far as he was concerned, he would not shrink from carrying out the decision of the

Council either from his natural affection for the King his brother, or even from fear of the danger to his own life.

Stephen, summoned to a Church Council to answer for his conduct, did not react with kingly outrage as his Norman predecessors would certainly have done. Instead, he came in person to Winchester, and although he did not actually appear before the court, he sent earls to enquire the reason why his presence had been requested. He was crisply reminded by the Legate that he owed obedience to Christ's Church, and that he had been guilty of a crime unheard-of in Christian lands. It was only among the heathen, he was told, that bishops were thrown into prison and stripped of their possessions. He advised the King, his brother, either to account for his conduct or else submit himself to the judgement of the Church.

The earls went away to report to the King and returned after an interval, this time accompanied by Aubrey de Vere, the King's Chamberlain, who had had considerable experience in legal matters. Aubrey was careful to take a moderate line, but none the less stressed the injuries the King had suffered at the hands of Bishop Roger, whose followers were unruly and constantly caused affrays at court – exactly as they had done at Oxford. He also alleged that the Bishop was a secret supporter of the King's enemies. He had been intending to give open support to the Empress Matilda, he said, and hand over all his castles to her if ever she should land in England. None the less, he had surrendered his castles to the King voluntarily in recognition of his misdeeds. There had been, it was true, some negligible amount of money in the Bishop's castles, but this, too, the Bishop had willingly handed over. It was a strange description of the Bishop's vast store of treasure. His strongest point, however, was the classic defence that the bishops had been arrested not as churchmen, servants of the Lord, but as paid officers of the Crown. The most significant thing of all about his speech, of course, was the fact that it was ever made, for by putting forward a defence, the King had, in effect, admitted the right of the court to judge him.

Bishop Roger began a spirited defence of his own conduct,

threatening that if he could not get justice from this court he would appeal to a higher one, presumably the Pope; but Bishop Henry merely observed with studied moderation that all the charges against the bishops should have been tried in an ecclesiastical court, and that in the meantime the bishops must have their property restored to them by the King.

Stephen managed to get the proceedings adjourned for a day or two until the Archbishop of Rouen, who was one of his firmest supporters, was present. The Archbishop took the line, when he arrived, that the onus lay on the bishops to prove that they were entitled to possess castles; and even if they were, it was their recognised duty, in such turbulent times, to hand over the keys to the King, if he demanded them. Aubrey de Vere followed this up by warning the bishops not to think lightly of appealing to Rome. If any of them left England in opposition to the King's wishes, they would find it easier to go than to return.

The Council broke up without taking any decisive action, since the King would not submit to censure on the part of the bishops and they shrank from any act of open hostility, such as excommunication. They knew that they would have been risking open violence, perhaps death, had they done more, since already 'swords were drawn'. Instead, Henry of Winchester and Archbishop Theobald went to have a personal interview with the King at which they flung themselves at his feet and begged him to take pity on the Church, and to take thought for his own soul and reputation. He paid them the courtesy of getting to his feet, but, as usual, the 'fair promises' he made them were never kept.

Outwardly, nothing had been changed by the Council, for Stephen kept the bishops' castles and their treasure, and the Council, by its lack of action, implicitly admitted Stephen's right to what he had taken. All the same, the affair marked a decisive change in Stephen's fortunes. Already a large number of the barons were in revolt against him, and a large number disaffected; now he had alienated the Church as well and imperilled the efficient administration of the kingdom by removing at one stroke the Justiciar, Roger of Salisbury, his son the Chancellor and his nephew Bishop Nigel of Ely, who was at the head of the Treasury.

The Empress Matilda and her brother were no doubt delighted at the new turn events had taken, for it was clear that the longed-for opportunity of making a successful invasion of England was becoming a practical possibility. In fact, they began their preparations for invasion at just about the time that the Council was sitting. They had still to solve the problem of finding a suitable port for the landing, however, and a safe place of refuge where they could establish themselves immediately afterwards.

As soon as the Council broke up, on 1 September 1139, Stephen had to hurry away to deal with yet another rebel, William de Mohun, who had fortified himself in Dunster castle and was raiding all the country round about. The castle, however, was almost impregnable and could only be taken after a prolonged siege, so Stephen left a force behind him to harry the defenders while he went on himself to Wareham, for he had received news that his old enemy Baldwin de Redvers had landed there, bringing with him a large body of supporters, and had seized Corfe castle.

Once again, there was little that Stephen could do, for the castle was well defended, and he was in any case distracted by rumours of a possible invasion by Matilda and Robert of Gloucester. He gave up the siege and hurried away, giving orders that all the ports were to be watched day and night so that the invaders might be intercepted at the first possible moment. In fact, they eluded his watch and managed to land successfully at Arundel on 30 September 1139.

This was of all things the news that Stephen had dreaded most. Until now the outbreaks of rebellion had been sporadic and had lacked a recognised overall leader. Even so, he had not been particularly successful in dealing with them. With Robert of Gloucester, a brave and experienced soldier, in England and ready to lead his enemies against him, and Empress Matilda, whose claim to the throne was at least as good as his own, also in the country, life was going to be very much more troublesome. It was not difficult to foresee an outburst of conscience occurring on every hand about the broken oath once Matilda was on the spot and claiming her rights. However, his line of action was clear; he put himself once more at the head of an army and marched on Arundel castle.

Bishop Roger, meanwhile, who in some measure had precipitated the crisis, had crept away to Salisbury, a dying man.

'They say', wrote William of Malmesbury, 'that he became ill through mental anguish at all that he had suffered at the hands of King Stephen. He had served King Henry well, and the King, for his part, had lavished on him estates, churches and whole abbeys of monks; he placed in his care the kingdom itself.' Roger had become wealthy and powerful beyond measure. And then, in his later years, 'Fortune, which had smiled on him for so long, had turned on him with bitter cruelty and struck him a blow like the sting in a scorpion's tail.'

Bishop Roger put his affairs in order as best he could, and then, when he knew that death could not be far away, he commanded that those treasures which still remained to him – 'coins in great heaps and vessels of hammered gold, delicately wrought' – should be piled up on the cathedral altar to keep them safe for the Church. But as he lay breathing away what little life remained to him, he saw them seized from the altar by King Stephen's men and taken away.

'I think it is his crowning misfortune,' wrote William of Malmesbury, 'and I grieve for it myself, that although he was a man greatly to be pitied, there was none to pity him.'

The great Bishop Roger of Salisbury died on 11 December 1139, and his remaining wealth, snatched by the King, wrought quite a transformation in Stephen's finances.

6 The Empress in England ❧

Henry 1's second Queen Adelisa, the 'fair maid of Brabant', had married again and was living with her husband William de Albini in Arundel castle, which Henry had given her for her own. Matilda had always been on good terms with her stepmother, and Adelisa had been particularly kind to her at the time when she was being forced into marriage with Geoffrey of Anjou. It is not, however, entirely clear whether Adelisa actually invited Matilda to land at Arundel, or whether she merely agreed to receive her when she had already arrived. At all events, she did allow Matilda and Robert of Gloucester to enter her castle, together with their small force of one hundred and forty knights.

Robert of Gloucester left almost immediately for Bristol with only twelve companions, leaving his wife and sister in the safe keeping, as he hoped, of Adelisa. Stephen, hearing what had happened, made an attempt to intercept Robert, which failed, as Robert kept to little-known byways. Stephen, therefore, returned to Arundel castle meaning to lay siege to it, but at this point Henry of Winchester, accompanied by a mounted bodyguard, joined his brother before the castle and gave Stephen advice which may, or may not, have been given in good faith. Would it not be sensible, he said, to allow Matilda to join her brother in Bristol? So long as Earl Robert and Matilda were kept apart, there were two centres of rebellion in the country, and the King's forces therefore had to be split. If they were allowed to come together in Bristol, the King could concentrate all his forces in one place and so crush the rebels. At the very least, the rebel

forces would be drawn away from London, and anybody who
planned to join them would be travelling away from, rather than
towards, the capital.

The advice had a certain plausibility, but it seems incredible, all the same, that Stephen should actually have taken it. A
hard-headed general would surely have preferred to have his
chief antagonist shut up in a castle, however impregnable, than
free to roam at large, to make plans and organise support. But
whether the advice was traitorous or not, Stephen did take it. He
went further and courteously gave Matilda an escort consist-
ing of Henry of Winchester and Count Waleran of Meulan, to
see her safely on her way. 'By allowing her to go,' comments
Orderic Vitalis, 'the King showed himself either simple-minded
or negligent . . . He had the chance to stifle a flame which was
potentially of great danger to him.' In fact, of course, he was
showing the same ill-judged generosity which he had shown in
the past.

It is tantalising that there is no record whatsoever of what may
have taken place between Henry of Winchester and Matilda as
they rode together on their journey. If Henry's advice had been
that of a traitor and intended to harm Stephen, then they had
plenty of opportunity to make plans and exchange information.
Whether a traitor or not, Henry was in no mood to be ultra-
loyal to his brother after the way he had been cheated, as he
thought, of the Archbishopric of Canterbury. There is even a
report that he had met Robert of Gloucester while he was on his
way to Bristol, had established friendly relations with him, and
then let him go on his way unmolested. It is more likely, however, that Henry had not reached the point of contemplating
actual desertion of his brother, but being the diplomat he was, he
may have welcomed the opportunity of getting on good terms
with Matilda in case the balance of power should change in the
future. Matilda, on her side, would have been foolish not to make
herself agreeable to a man of such power and influence; but then
sometimes she was foolish. And, of course, Henry was her cousin,
he had been one of the bishops who had sworn to recognise her

as Queen, and he had broken his vow. It could have gone either way, but it is certainly a possibility that something was said or agreed between them which had an influence on their relationship during their brief alliance two years later.

Waleran of Meulan, of course, was with them at the start, and at this time he was certainly one of Stephen's firmest supporters, although he did desert him later. He left them, however, at Calne and they travelled on alone.

Whatever the events of the journey, Matilda was safely delivered into the care of her brother at Bristol. Robert had one piece of good news to report to her, for he had met Brian fitzCount on the way to Bristol, who had known Matilda well in the old days at the court of King Henry i. He was the castellan of Wallingford castle which, from its situation on the route from London to Oxford and the West Country, was of great strategic importance, and he had at once declared his determination to throw off his allegiance to Stephen and to support Matilda.

She was also joined by Miles of Gloucester, one of her father's 'new men', who, like Brian fitzCount, was experienced in warfare. 'He came to me as quickly as he could at Bristol,' recorded Matilda. 'He recognised me as "lady" and rightful heir to the realm of England, and he escorted me from Bristol to Gloucester. There he paid homage to me as my liege man against all others.'

Miles had originally been sheriff of Gloucester, like his father before him, but he had later become sheriff of Staffordshire and castellan of the King's castle at Gloucester. Stephen, after his succession, had issued a charter confirming him in the possession of his lands and honours, and had given him the additional privilege of holding Gloucester direct from the King instead of from Robert of Gloucester. He had not, however, won his loyalty

Stephen, after gravely handicapping his cause by letting Matilda go free and allowing his enemies to establish themselves in three strong points, Bristol, Wallingford and Gloucester, became very busy trying to retrieve the situation. 'Undismayed', so it was said, by the 'tide of evils' flowing in on him from every side, he collected his forces to do battle with his enemies. First he made for Wallingford. The barons who accompanied him were, as usual, ready with dispiriting, if not disingenuous, counsel. Wallingford castle, they told him, was so strongly fortified that it was impossible to launch a successful assault on it from any direction at all. It was also so well stocked with provisions that it could hold out not merely for months, but for years. The garrison consisted of picked men and Stephen would be exposed to attack not only from them, but from other enemy forces as well which were pressing in on every side.

Either Brian fitzCount had succeeded in making the castle genuinely impregnable, or Stephen was receiving, not for the first time, slanted advice. But he did what they told him. He built two forts, manned them with sufficient troops to keep up a blockade and then went off to Trowbridge. On the way he captured two minor castles; but while he was thus occupied, Miles of Gloucester made a dash for Wallingford, attacked the troops which Stephen had left behind him, captured or killed every single man and flattened the 'forts' which Stephen had erected. Probably they were no more than wooden structures put up on the top of mounds, but even so their destruction was a blow for Stephen.

Satisfied with this highly successful expedition, Miles returned to Gloucester, where Matilda's supporters were gathering. Among them were the 'disinherited' – those men whose lands and honours had been taken from them to satisfy the never-ceasing demands of Stephen's followers. Matilda herself was also at Gloucester, and there she received the homage of those who accepted her as Queen.

At Trowbridge Stephen was faced once more with a seemingly impregnable castle and he made little progress in his attempts to take it. Once again he turned aside, his barons this time warning him that Robert of Gloucester was collecting an army and might attack him at any moment. He would do better, they told him, to go back to London, rally his forces, and wait for a moment when fortune seemed more favourable. Stephen, ever pliable, agreed, but paused on the way to leave a garrison at Devizes to harass the defenders of Trowbridge.

Miles of Gloucester, meanwhile, had returned to the West Country and chose this moment to make an attack on the city of Worcester. It was what the inhabitants had been dreading.

'While all these direful events were going on,' wrote a monk of Worcester, 'sad tidings' came to the ears of the citizens. Their city was to be sacked, all its riches taken and the city itself burnt to the ground. The men of Worcester, in high alarm, had consulted together and had decided that there was nothing they could do but rely on divine protection. So they carried all their belongings into the cathedral church, and settled down there themselves. 'Oh miserable sight!' exclaimed the Chronicler. 'Behold the house of God which should have been entered with sacrifices now looking like a furniture Depository! Behold the mother church of the diocese become an inn!' There were so many chests, sacks, boxes and goods of all sorts piled up high that the monks and priests could hardly find room to move and their 'holy chanting' had to compete with the howling of infants and the sobbing of mothers. 'Oh misery of miseries to behold!' The high altar was stripped of its ornaments, the cross taken down, and the statue of the Virgin Mary hidden away for safety. Everything, in fact, which was movable or of value – curtains, copes, stoles, vestments as well as articles of silver and precious metals – all were concealed in case the enemy should come without warning and strip them of their treasures. The holy offices of the church had to be kept to a minimum and conducted amid a rabble of noisy refugees. Misery of miseries indeed.

And at daybreak on 7 November, while the monks were saying prime, the expected disaster happened. A great army, 'strong and valiant', marched in from the south to attack the city. 'We, however,' continued the Chronicler, 'in our terror and anxiety for the treasures of the sanctuary, put on albs, took up the relics of Oswald our most benignant patron, tolled the bells, and then marched in humble procession out of the church.'

The first attack was launched against a strongly defended

position on the southern part of the city near the castle, and such a determined resistance was put up by the citizens that the attack failed. It was then switched to the north of the city, and here there was no resistance at all; presumably an attack had not been expected from that quarter. A disorderly rabble of soldiers burst into the city and began setting fire to the buildings. Most of the buildings in those days were of wood and a fire always threatened to be a major disaster, but a large part of the city was none the less saved. The possessions of the citizens fared worse, for the invaders made off with a vast booty not only of household goods, but oxen, sheep, cattle and horses as well. A number of prisoners were also taken, and these were 'bound in couples like hounds and carried away into a miserable captivity'. At last, the 'furious and drunken rabble' left the city. 'Woe is me! Grievous deeds were done on the first day of winter.'

The Earl of Worcester arrived a little later, and seeing the dreadful destruction in the city, he was deeply grieved; but he proceeded to assuage his grief by going off and doing worse to nearby Sudeley. 'And if it be enquired what the earl did there,' wrote the Chronicler, 'the answer must be such as should hardly be handed down to memory.' He came marching back next day feeling greatly lightened in spirit and bringing with him an enormous booty.

If Miles's idea in attacking Worcester had been to divert Stephen from a new assault on Wallingford, it succeeded, for Stephen came hurrying to Worcester at the head of a large army and arrived there at the end of November. Miles, however, had long since left and there was nothing for Stephen to do but view the damage and commiserate with the citizens.

From the point of view of the ordinary people, it made little difference which side had the upper hand, for it was always they who suffered. Knights and nobles were seldom killed in battle. They were well protected by their helmets and their armour, and it was in any case far more profitable for their enemies to capture and hold them for ransom than to kill them. It was ordinary people, the small townsmen, the tillers of the soil, who were the victims of both sides. They suffered when the besieged garrison of a castle laid waste the country for miles around so as to leave nothing for an invading army to live on, and they suffered equally when the invaders, in their turn, destroyed and burnt everything that was left, so as to make sure that no supplies could reach the besieged.

With hostile bands of men roaming the country, law and order broke down, and everyone was open to attack. Gone was the 'good peace' of King Henry's reign when a man could safely bear his burden of gold and silver from one end of the country to the other. The chroniclers of the time join in a chorus of despair. Everywhere castles sprang up which were centres of violence. 'The garrisons drove off the sheep and cattle,' said William of Malmesbury. 'They seized any man who was thought to possess money and tortured him until he promised them whatever they wanted. They plundered the houses of simple husbandmen, taking away even their beds; the men themselves they flung into prison. Many died under torture. It was terrible indeed to see England, once the especial home of tranquillity, reduced to such a pitch of misery.' 'There was no peace anywhere,' wrote another. 'Nothing but lamentation, grief and horror.' 'Slaughter, fire and rapine, cries of anguish and horror on every side,' recorded Henry of Huntingdon. As for the King, he went on, it was of no consequence where he spent Christmas or Easter, for all that had once made the court splendid had long since passed away.

Stephen's Christmas, in fact, had been profitably spent in Salisbury that year, acquiring the late Bishop's treasure, but money was soon short again, and once more the coinage was debased, so much so this time that it was said that out of ten shillings, hardly twelve pennies were up to standard. This had been done on the King's orders, for he was by this time so short of funds that he had not enough to pay for the upkeep of his own knights. 'So everything in England was up for sale,' wrote William of Malmesbury, 'Churches and abbeys were put on the market, no longer in secret, but quite openly.'

The next year, 1140, was a year of trial for England, a year of chaos, and bloodshed, and treachery, each man fighting for himself and each castle becoming the centre of a little kingdom. Nigel of Ely, still hostile to Stephen for his treachery at Oxford and for his treatment of his relatives, rebelled early in the year. He engaged mercenary soldiers, desperate men ready for any deed of violence, and began attacking those of his neighbours who supported the King. Stephen marched to their help, but Nigel was entrenched in a very strong position. Ely was still an island at this time, and it was protected by fenland on every side. There was only one approach to it and that was over a causeway leading straight to the castle. The only possible way of invading this natural stronghold, so Stephen's advisers told him, was by collecting a number of boats and using them as a bridge.

He followed this advice, and he and his army managed to make the crossing; they even succeeded in capturing the castle. The Bishop, however, had already made his escape and he got safely to Gloucester, where he joined Matilda and her party.

The situation soon became more confused than ever, with divided loyalties and switches of attachment. A man called Robert fitzHubert, a sadistic character who boasted that he had seen eighty monks burnt and enjoyed it, attacked and took the castle of Devizes by a strategem. He was nominally a supporter of the Earl of Gloucester, but was really playing his own hand and acting against him. Unfortunately for him, he grew too ambitious and decided that he would like to add the castle of Marlborough to his sphere of influence. Accordingly, he sent a message to the knight in charge of it, John fitzGilbert, suggesting that a little talk might be to their mutual advantage. John received the suggestion with apparent enthusiasm and asked Robert into his castle, as dangerous an invitation as that of the spider to the fly, for he immediately threw Robert into a dungeon, then rushed out and captured most of his bodyguard. The few who managed to escape fled back to Devizes.

Robert of Gloucester then intervened. He went to Marlborough, collected the traitorous Robert from his captor, marched him off to Devizes, and there hanged him in full view of the castle garrison. They eventually surrendered – not, however, to Robert of Gloucester, but to one of Stephen's supporters.

In June, Stephen had to hurry off to East Anglia, this time because of trouble with Hugh Bigod. Meanwhile Robert of Gloucester was busy making an attack on Nottingham. There was little serious resistance and the attackers swept through the city, plundering and looting as they went.

One wealthy burgher was forced to take a party of marauders to his cellar to show them where he kept his gold and other valuables. He waited quietly until they were thoroughly absorbed in the task of opening his treasure chests, then crept out and slammed the door on them. After that, he set his house on fire and burnt it to the ground, pillagers and all. Unfortunately the city went up in flames as well, for the fire spread and hardly a building was left intact. Those who had fled to the churches were engulfed by the fire, for they hesitated too long before escaping, torn between fear of being burnt alive and fear of the soldiers outside. In the end, it was the fire that killed most of them, and those few who escaped the flames were led away in chains to Gloucester.

And so it went on. In the summer of 1140 Bishop Henry of Winchester made an attempt to arrange some sort of compromise peace between his brother and the Empress Matilda. A meeting was organised near Bath with Robert of Gloucester as the chief representative of Matilda on the one hand, and Bishop Henry himself, the Archbishop of Canterbury and Stephen's Queen on the other. 'But vainly, vainly I say,' wrote William of Malmesbury, 'did they spend their words and their time for they went away with no peace made.'

The Empress, however, appears to have been more inclined to be reasonable than Stephen, for she declared that for her part, she would have no fear of appealing to the judgement of the Church, while Stephen was not prepared to admit that his right to rule should be put in question at all. Henry of Winchester must none the less have felt that there was still some chance of an agreement, for he crossed to France in September and held a conference with the French King Louis VII, Count Theobald of Blois and various churchmen. It is not known exactly what was agreed between them, but he seems to have come back towards the end of November with a proposed set of conditions which might have brought peace if only they could have been translated into practice. Once more, the Empress and her party were prepared to come to an agreement, but the King prevaricated and put off making any decision, until at last the whole affair came to nothing.

Henry of Winchester then kept himself aloof, and waited and watched to see how things would go; 'for what is the point', asked William of Malmesbury, 'of trying to swim against a raging torrent? It is the height of folly to strive with all one's might and in the end win nothing but hostility.'

7 The Battle of Lincoln

Ranulf, Earl of Chester, was one of the most powerful barons in the country, for he owned such vast areas of land, chiefly in the north-west, that they amounted almost to a kingdom in themselves. He was inclined to be hostile to Stephen because he had a claim, through his father, to the large and important 'honour' of Carlisle, and he was furious that Stephen had made it over to the Scots; so furious, in fact, that he made a plot to kidnap Prince Henry of Scotland. It might have succeeded if Stephen's Queen had not got wind of it and taken steps to prevent it.

Ranulf had none the less avoided committing himself to supporting Empress Matilda, in spite of the fact that he was married to Robert of Gloucester's daughter, as he had grievances against their side as well. He was only interested in supporting his own advancement, and he concocted a plan with his half-brother William of Roumare, who had inherited large estates in Lincolnshire, to join up their territories and erect a string of fortresses which should stretch from one side of England to the other.

Stephen may have known nothing in detail of these plans, but he was none the less a little nervous of these powerful brothers, and he was anxious to propitiate them if he could. It was easier for him to offer concessions in East Anglia than in the north, where any gifts might cause offence to the Scottish king, so probably at some time towards the end of 1140 he conferred the title of Earl of Cambridge on William of Roumare. He also gave some title or distinction to Ranulf as well, although it is not known exactly what it was.

Hoping that he had now won their good will, Stephen went off to London, while Ranulf and his brother stayed behind in Lincoln. They were not in the least mollified by Stephen's high-sounding honours, which meant little to them; on the contrary, they were busy putting the finishing touches to a plan which they had almost certainly worked out some time before.

Ranulf was a bold and determined man who was not afraid of a quarrel. If he had brought off his scheme of kidnapping Prince Henry of Scotland, he would have involved himself in a quarrel with two very powerful men – two kings, in fact. He was not afraid. He was afraid of nothing and had no intention of putting up with the loss of what he felt to be his rightful claim to Carlisle, whether it meant an all-out battle with the King or not.

Ranulf and his brother had decided to seize the castle of Lincoln as a first step in their campaign to establish their rights. They were to do it, not by force, but by a ruse. Soon after Stephen had left, at a time when most of the castle garrison were outside the gates amusing themselves in one way or another, Ranulf and his brother sent their wives into the castle. They appeared to have arrived for no particular reason but to pass the time of day, and they stayed on chatting and laughing with the wife of the knight who was the official guardian of the castle tower. Soon Ranulf strolled in and joined them. No suspicion was aroused by his arrival, for he was not wearing armour and he was accompanied by only three soldiers. It was assumed that he had merely come to fetch his wife.

Suddenly, however, he and his men snatched up pieces of wood, metal bars – any weapon that came to hand – and made a fierce attack on the royal guard, driving them out of the castle. They then let Ranulf's brother inside, together with a band of armed men, and so installed themselves in the citadel.

All had gone exactly according to plan. It was a plan, however, that does not seem to have been thought out very far ahead, for they did nothing more than settle down in the castle. Even then, they were short-sighted enough to treat the citizens somewhat harshly and they even managed to offend Bishop Alexander of

Lincoln, who had no reason to feel kindly towards Stephen. They annoyed him so seriously that he joined with the citizens in sending a message to Stephen asking him to come to their rescue. If he were quick, they told Stephen, he would be able to take the two earls by surprise, surround the castle and get possession of it as the earls were completely off their guard and quite unprepared for an attack.

Stephen was very surprised that his two 'dearest friends' should have turned against him, and so soon after he had been showering them with honours. The invitation, however, was hard to refuse, for a successful attack against these two powerful men would strengthen his own position enormously. He was keeping the Christmas festival in London when he got the message, but, without wasting a moment, he mustered an army and arrived outside Lincoln in the first week of January. The citizens welcomed him into their city, and he began his preparations to besiege the castle.

Stephen had moved very quickly, but even so news of his approach reached the two earls in time for Ranulf, 'the youngest, the most active, and the most daring', to get out of the castle before it was surrounded. He escaped with only one or two companions, but seemed at first to have no very clear idea what to do next. In fact, he did the obvious thing. He made for his own lands in Cheshire, and from there sent the news of his breach with the King to his father-in-law, Robert of Gloucester. He appealed to him for help, help not only for himself, but for his wife, Robert's daughter, left behind in the castle, perhaps in danger. He declared that he was ready to recognise Matilda and would pay her homage if Robert came to his aid.

Robert did not hesitate. He had been trying to persuade Ranulf to support Matilda for some time, and he must have been delighted at securing such a powerful new ally. He and Miles of Gloucester summoned their supporters, among them a large party of the 'disinherited' who were 'inflamed to battle by grief for all that they had lost', and they set off for Lincoln, joining Ranulf's army somewhere on the way.

Matilda, prohibited by her sex from joining in battle, was left behind to endure frustration and suspense. She would probably have preferred to fight. Arnulf, Bishop of Lisieux, once said of her that she was a woman who had 'nothing of the woman about her', and she was well known for her 'intrepid' spirit. As a woman, however, she lacked the sheer physical strength to join in the rough and tumble of medieval battle and she had to stay quietly in Miles's castle of Gloucester and wait for news.

It must have been a bitter march across the breadth of England in the cold of January and in a season of particularly severe storms. Their route is not entirely clear, but they seem to have approached the city along the Foss-way, which enters Lincoln by means of a bridge over the river Witham. To attempt to cross the bridge itself would, of course, have been far too dangerous a procedure for an army, so when they came near to the city they turned westwards, making for a ford which they knew to exist. In the event, however, it seemed to have disappeared. The rains had been very heavy and the river was so swollen that there was no sign of it, nothing but an unbroken sheet of fast-flowing water.

'This is just as I would have chosen it!' exclaimed Robert of Gloucester. 'Once across, there will be no going back. We shall have to conquer or die.'

Without hesitation, he plunged into the rushing water, Ranulf did the same, and all their followers after them. Stephen had posted a guard by the ford, evidently guessing that they might attempt to cross the river at that point, but it was easily overcome and Robert's army advanced to the south-western outskirts of the city.

Stephen, meanwhile, had been asking advice from his barons as to what he ought to do, and as usual their advice was depressing and negative. Some of them strongly advised him to leave a force to defend the town while he himself went away to recruit a large and really formidable army. He could then return, as opportunity offered, and take the castle by storm. Others recommended him to remember that it was a holy day – it was 2 February, the feast of the Purification of the Virgin, the Holy Mother of God – and they said that it would be wrong to engage in battle on such a day. His best course would be to send messengers to the approaching army and try to arrange some sort of truce.

Stephen was not happy about either of these proposals. It may be that he was influenced by the memory of his father's disgrace after he ran away from the siege of Antioch. The circumstances were strikingly similar; his father, too, had been taking part in a siege, and had then found himself besieged in his turn. His father had refused a fight and had run away. This Stephen would *not* do. On no account would he stain his reputation by the ignominy of flight.

On the morning of 2 February 1141 Stephen heard mass. There are slightly differing accounts of exactly what happened, but all versions agree that the omens were distinctly sinister. King Stephen was holding in his hand, according to custom, a consecrated wax candle, and just as he was about to place it in the hands of Bishop Alexander, he dropped it – another chronicler says that it broke of itself – and it fell to the ground. The broken candle was regarded as a sign that the King would fall from power on that day. In addition, the chain by which the pyx containing the Blessed Sacrament was hanging broke and the pyx fell on the altar just as the Bishop was celebrating the office. Another version of the story, perhaps wise after the event, goes on to say that although the candle was broken and the flame extinguished, the King kept it in his hand. The candle was then stuck together and it was re-lighted, a symbol that although Stephen might fall into the hands of his enemies, he would not in the end lose his kingdom.

These unlucky events occurred in the presence of a number of witnesses, and given the tendency of the times to look for signs and portents – a rain of blood, dragons in the sky, children born green – it cannot have made an encouraging start to the day. The story would have spread quickly through the men of the army and it may even have been a factor in undermining their will to fight. There is no record of what Stephen himself said or thought, but even the least superstitious of men would as soon have been

The Great Seal of Empress Matilda

The coronation of Henry v, Matilda's first husband, as Holy Roman Emperor by Pope Paschal (right) depicted in a twelfth-century manuscript

Geoffrey of Anjou (from an enamel plaque, originally in Le Mans Cathedral)

The ruins of the château of Falaise

The castle of Angers

ABOVE A fleet crossing the English Channel (Bayeux tapestry, early twelfth century)

ABOVE Dinner is served (Bayeux tapestry)

BELOW A typical medieval siege, here of Dinan (Bayeux tapestry)

ABOVE Contemporary illustration of weaving from the Psalter of Eadivine, monk of Christ Church, Canterbury

BELOW Soldiers besieging Jerusalem in a manuscript of the twelfth to thirteenth century

ABOVE Illuminated initial from the Kelso Charter showing King David of Scotland and his son, Malcolm

BELOW A reconstruction of medieval Devizes Castle

RIGHT Bristol Castle as it was thought to be in 1138, from which Stephen was released in 1141

LEFT Reliquary of the True Cross presented by Matilda to the Abbey of Valasse

BELOW Dominating the Thames valley was the important stronghold of Oxford Castle

MATILDA IMPERATRIX

Regis Henrici filia et Anglie Domina Justiciariis vicecomitibus
z ministris z ministris suis totius Anglie z portui z Sariis Salut
Concedo Burgensibus meis de Divisis ꝙ pro servitio z
suo sint quieti de Theolon Passag z Lestag z omni alia z
consuetudine p totam terram meam et p portuo maris Et volo
z precipio ꝙ ipi et heredes sui z oia mercat sua meam firmam
pacem habeant et sup hor nemo eos usquam iniuste distur bet
super x li forisfactur Teste Epo Eli apud Radinges

Early seventeenth-century representation
of Matilda from the Devizes Charter

without evil omens on a day of crisis. He had made up his mind, however, that he must face the enemy, so he put on his armour and prepared himself for battle.

Robert of Gloucester and his army seem to have made their way round the foot of the hill on which the citadel stands, and they were drawn up on a stretch of comparatively dry ground. Above them, they could see the stark outline of the castle where Ranulf's wife and brother were still holding out.

There now ensued a dispute as to precedence, for Ranulf of Chester claimed the right to be in the forefront of the battle. According to one account, Ranulf thanked Robert of Gloucester and the other barons for taking part in what was essentially his own private quarrel, and for being prepared to fight in a battle for which he was responsible. He would 'hew a path', he said, through the centre of King Stephen's army and it would be for them to follow him. He had no doubt that victory would be theirs and the King's army routed.

Robert of Gloucester, however, would have none of this. The affair, he said, was something far greater than a personal dispute. 'The King has usurped the crown,' he declared. 'He has broken the oath that he swore to recognise my sister, and many thousands have died in the chaos and disorder that has spread throughout this land.'

He reminded them that there could be no retreat over the marshes they had just crossed; there could be no safety in flight. The only way they could go was forward into the city, forward to victory, relying on their own courage and high hearts, and on God's justice.

It was a rousing speech, which was received with great enthusiasm, and the men of his army raised their arms and shouted, swearing that they would never retreat. The army was then formed in battle array with the 'disinherited' forming the front line, Ranulf of Chester in command of the second line which, was to fight on foot, and Robert of Gloucester commanding the third line. 'A dreadful and hideous band of Welshmen', which formed part of Ranulf's army, was drawn up on the flanks.

D

Stephen, too, wanted to encourage his army with a rousing
eve-of-battle address, but he had rather a feeble voice which could
not be trusted to carry, so Baldwin fitzGilbert was deputed to
make the speech for him.

He exhorted the men of their army to consider three things:
the justice of their cause, their numbers and their exceptional
valour. As for the justice of their cause, they were fighting for
their rightful King against subjects who had taken up arms
against him; and God, naturally, would be on their side.

He then spoke slightingly of the Earl of Gloucester, with 'the
mouth of a lion and the heart of a hare'. The Earl of Chester was
daring, it was true, but he was rash and unlikely to carry any
project through to a good end. The Welsh were nothing but an
ill-conditioned mob, and all the other barons were turncoats or
traitors.

He was just getting into his stride when the trumpets sounded
from Earl Robert's army and they heard shouting and the
thunder of hooves. Battle was upon them. It was a battle immensely important in its results, and Stephen, at least, covered
himself with honour, wiping out for ever any possible charge of
cowardice; but it was not an heroic affair in any other regard.

The 'disinherited' made the first charge, scattering Stephen's
front lines, while the Welshmen launched a vigorous attack on his
flank. The Welsh were driven back by William of Ypres and his
men, but Ranulf of Chester moved in to the attack, and in a
moment the battle was virtually over. It was a rout. The first to
run away was William of Ypres, a professional soldier and until
then regarded as a man of unusual courage. When his men broke
and fled, he went with them. Alan of Richmond and his men
lasted scarcely longer. In a moment, the whole of the King's
cavalry was in headlong retreat, riding for their lives in panic
and despair. Waleran of Meulan fled, so did Gilbert of Clare
and William of Warenne, famous names of supposedly valiant
knights. They fled almost before the battle had well begun; but
not Stephen. Alone, with his personal followers, his foot soldiers,
and perhaps a few of the men of Lincoln who may have joined

the battle, Stephen stood and fought. 'He stood like a lion, the bravest of the brave, fearing the attack of none.'

Again and again, men of the opposing army flung themselves at him; and were driven back. The battle raged about him – the clash of sword on helmet, the screams of the wounded, the whinnying of the horses and the thud of hooves. His enemies set on Stephen as though 'storming a castle'; and still he fought back, doing terrible slaughter.

Ranulf of Chester, with his men-at-arms behind him, flung himself at the King. The King's sword shattered in his hand, but a man of Lincoln, who was fighting beside him, gave him a Danish battle-axe in its place, perhaps a more terrible weapon still, and Stephen laid about him with that. 'Grinding his teeth and foaming at the mouth like a wild boar', he brought the axe down with all his force on Ranulf's helmet. Ranulf was knocked to his knees and crouched helpless in the mud. But at that moment someone – nobody knows who it was – flung a stone at Stephen which struck him on the head. He, too, fell to the ground, and a knight, William of Cahagnes, seized his helmet and, pulling it from his head, shouted, 'I've got the King!' *captured*.

The battle was over. Stephen made formal surrender to his cousin, Robert of Gloucester, and he was led away, a prisoner. It seemed that not only the battle but the war was at an end.

The carnage, however, was not over. The men of Lincoln, knowing what their fate must be since it was they who had sent a message to the King asking him to come, fled for their lives. In a panic they abandoned wives, houses and all that they possessed in a wild desire to escape and get away at any cost. They rushed down to the river and crowded on to the boats which were moored there, but as they pushed off from the bank, others kept leaping on board, landing on top of those already in the boats, which, overloaded, began to sink. Almost everyone in the boats was drowned, perhaps five hundred of the leading citizens of Lincoln.

None the less, they may have had a more merciful death than those they left behind in the city, for Ranulf and his men had entered Lincoln by this time and they butchered every man, woman, and child they could find.

Stephen, meanwhile, was being treated with the greatest consideration and kindness by Earl Robert, who would not allow him to be exposed to the slightest discourtesy of any kind. Stephen felt his humilation sharply enough, all the same, and as his arms were taken from him, he kept lamenting his fate.

'This dreadful disaster has come upon me as a punishment for my sins,' he declared. 'But I am not the only sinner. They, too, have committed sin who broke their feudal oaths, forgot the duty and loyalty they owe me as their liege lord, and came out in rebellion against me.'

The clergy, the monks and the common people grieved for the downfall of the King because he was 'not overproud, but courteous and friendly to everyone who kept the peace'. If only his treacherous barons had made it possible, they maintained, he would have been a generous protector and a friend to all the people of his country.

The trouble was, of course, that however kind and friendly, he was simply not cut out to be a king. 'He is the King of peace,' wrote a contemporary, 'but would that he were the King of vigour and justice as well.'

Matilda, waiting in suspense in Gloucester for news of the battle, must have experienced every crisis of anxiety through the long weeks which intervened. It is not known in what form the news finally reached her – whether a messenger was sent on to her in advance to tell her of the victory, or whether her first knowledge of what had happened came with the arrival of Earl Robert and his prisoner on 9 February 1141. But it was news more splendid than she could possibly have imagined, for here was victory indeed, decisive and undeniable. The King was in her hands, his forces broken.

What sort of meeting can it have been between Matilda and Stephen, the first for many years, the first since they had been on terms of close friendship, if nothing more, at King Henry's court? It is unlikely that Matilda felt any tenderness for Stephen, even if she remembered her feelings of long ago. Probably resentment outweighed everything else, but if so, she did not allow it to influence her, for Stephen was treated with consideration during his first weeks of captivity, which were spent in Bristol castle.

The effect of this sudden reversal of fortune on Matilda was dramatic. She was transported with delight, she was overjoyed, everything she wanted seemed to have fallen into her hands at once. And her character seemed to change for the worse as her fortunes improved. 'Instead of the modest and gentle demeanour proper to her sex', wrote a contemporary chronicler, she developed a 'scornful and arrogant air' and began to behave as though she were already Queen. She was certainly determined to become one, with all ceremony, at the earliest possible moment.

This was not something which could be achieved overnight, however, for although Stephen was in captivity, many of his adherents were still at large and showing every disposition to go on fighting. His Queen Matilda, brave and resolute as usual, was desperately trying to raise an army in her rallying ground of Kent, and she had already been joined by William of Ypres, anxious, perhaps, to atone for his desertion of the King at Lincoln, and by Waleran of Meulan and a number of others.

The first and most important thing for Matilda to do was to gain the support of the bishops, who had, on the whole, been holding aloof from the conflict during the last year. In particular, it was vital for her to win over the powerful Bishop of Winchester, the Papal Legate, her own cousin and the King's brother. Henry, however, was in a tricky position; if he joined Matilda, he would probably gain in honour and prestige, while continued support of the King's cause seemed to offer little prospect of success. On the other hand, it was difficult to put a good face on the desertion of a brother in distress.

Matilda sent a message to him asking him to receive her in his cathedral at Winchester, both as King Henry's daughter and England's Queen. He temporised by arranging to meet her outside Winchester, almost certainly at Wherwell, near Andover.

Their meeting place is said to have been on flat and open ground,
so it was probably at the foot of the hill which juts up above the
river Test. It took place on Sunday 2 March on a dull, wet, windy
day, with frequent bursts of rain which, so it was said, seemed to
presage a new and gloomy turn of fortune. All seemed to go well,
however, and terms were agreed between them. On her side, she
promised that he should be her adviser on all matters of importance, and that he should control the appointment of bishops and
senior churchmen. In return, he would allow her to enter
Winchester, where the royal treasury and the crown were housed,
and he would himself receive her in his cathedral, so giving an
open demonstration of his change of allegiance.

The next day she entered Winchester with all pomp and ceremony. Ecclesiastics and laymen alike came out to meet her and
escort her into the city, including two convents of monks and one
of nuns, all chanting praises as they came. Bishop Henry rode on
her right hand as they came into the city, and Bernard, Bishop of
St David's, on her left. Other bishops had gathered to show their
new allegiance, among them Bishops Alexander of Lincoln and
Nigel of Ely, old enemies of Stephen since the affair at Oxford,
Robert of Hereford, Robert of Bath, and perhaps Seffrid of
Chichester. A number of abbots were also present, including
Gilbert Foliot of Gloucester, who was to become prominent
later as Bishop of Hereford and then of London. Afterwards, at a
public meeting in the market place, she was hailed by the people
as 'lady and queen'. This was at Bishop Henry's insistence. It
was all very pleasing to Matilda, and it must have been a moment
of supreme joy to her when the royal crown was at last placed in
her hands. The royal treasure, however, turned out to be something of a disappointment since it was practically all gone.

Theobald of Canterbury was *not* there, but he arrived a few
days later and met the Empress at Wilton, near Salisbury. He did
not at once follow the Bishop of Winchester's example in giving
his allegiance to her, but made difficulties of conscience. He could
not, he said, swear allegiance to her as 'lady' (the title given to a
Queen before she has been crowned) without first consulting the

King. To act otherwise would be unworthy of his good name and of his office. Matilda, in spite of her new haughtiness, does not seem to have made any difficulties, and she allowed Theobald, together with most of the other bishops and a number of laymen, to go to the King in Bristol and ask his permission to change sides 'as the times constrained them'.

It must have been a strange meeting, almost impossible to picture: the imprisoned King, with everything lost, as it seemed, receiving the suppliant bishops with their curious desire to ask his kind permission to betray him. Stephen, however, even in these distressing circumstances, lived up to the highest standards of knightly chivalry. With great courtesy he told them that they must do whatever seemed to them best.

8 A Very Brief Authority ✌

Henry of Winchester summoned a 'Legatine Council' to meet at Winchester on 7 April 1141. The fact that it was a Legatine Council meant that Henry, as Papal Legate, would preside instead of Theobald, Archbishop of Canterbury, normally his superior in the hierarchy of the Church. It is not certain whether Matilda was present at the Council, or even in Winchester, although it seems probable that she would have been. It is not at all clear, in fact, what her movements were during March and April of this year, although she is known to have visited Reading at some point, for it was there that she received Robert d'Oilly, the castellan of Oxford castle, who did homage to her. A number of barons who had previously supported Stephen also transferred their allegiance to her sometime during this period.

The Council of Winchester was fairly well attended, although the proceedings began with the reading of letters of excuse from those who were absent. William of Malmesbury, who was there, gives a detailed description of the proceedings. 'I will not deny posterity', he wrote, 'a full account of all that was done, for I remember it very clearly indeed.'

Henry of Winchester made a speech on the Tuesday, the second day. He said that they were met together to confer on the state of the country, which was in grave danger and near to shipwreck. In the days of his uncle King Henry, England had been the haven of peace to an extraordinary degree, for no man, whatever his position, had dared to stir up trouble. Even neighbouring kings and princes had been influenced by King Henry's example and had cultivated peace.

Some years before his death, he went on, that same king had asked all the bishops and nobles of England to swear on oath that his daughter, his only surviving child, should succeed to his kingdom of England and his Duchy of Normandy at his death, provided that no son was born to him in the meantime. 'Fate was cruel to my uncle,' said the Bishop, 'for he died in Normandy leaving no male heir behind him.'

Here Henry came to a tricky part of his speech, for he had to explain how it was, after giving this solemn oath to recognise Matilda, he and the other bishops had in fact recognised Stephen. He was not able to find any very convincing excuse and his speech is distinctly thin at this point.

'It seemed that there might be a long wait before the King's daughter would arrive,' he said. 'She was living in Normandy and there were delays about her coming over to England. The peace of the country had to be safeguarded . . .' He stumbled on. 'And so my brother was allowed to become king.'

He had more awkward explanations to give. He admitted his own part in the negotiations over Stephen's accession: that he had stood guarantor between his brother and God, that he had given his word that his brother would honour and exalt Holy Church, and that he would maintain those laws that were good and do away with those that were bad.

'It is painful for me to remember,' he confessed, 'and shameful to have to put into words, what sort of a King my brother showed himself to be.' He had failed to exact just retribution from those who broke the law, the peace of the country had been shattered almost at once, bishops had been arrested and stripped of their possessions, high offices of the Church had been put up for sale and churches pillaged. The King had listened to the counsel of evil men, and had treated the advice of good and wise men as of little worth.

'You yourselves know how often I appealed to him,' he said, 'sometimes in person and sometimes through the bishops, but I gained nothing by my efforts but hatred.'

Now he came to the most difficult part of all.

'Naturally it is my duty to love my mortal brother,' he said carefully, 'but as any right thinking man will agree, it is my duty to pay far greater regard to the interests of my immortal Father. Since, therefore, the judgement of God has been executed against my brother, in that he has been allowed to fall into the hands of powerful men – a thing, of course, of which I knew nothing at the time – I, as Legate, have invited you to meet here so that the kingdom, left without a ruler, may not falter and fail.'

This matter, he said, had been the subject of confidential discussions the day before among the greater part of the clergy of England, who had a special prerogative in the matter of choosing and consecrating a king.

'We choose', he concluded, 'as Lady of England and Normandy the daughter of a King who was a notable peacemaker, a King glorious, rich and good, a King who has had no equal in our times. We choose her and we promise her our loyalty and support.'

He finished to modest applause, and those who failed to applaud at least gave no sign of disagreement. Henry of Winchester had, in fact, surmounted a difficult hurdle and he had certainly achieved a very complete revenge for the humiliations Stephen had been foolish enough to inflict on him. He had also made a somewhat astonishing claim on behalf of the Church to a 'special prerogative' in the making of a king.

Nobody spoke against him or raised the ticklish matter of the oaths they had all sworn to Stephen and the homage they had paid him, an unpleasant fact to digest, even though Stephen had so handsomely released them from their obligations to him; perhaps all the more unpleasant in view of his generosity.

Henry then went on to inform them that he had invited representatives of the city of London to join them. This was a *de facto* recognition of the power the Londoners were able to exert and which made them almost the equal of a tenant-in-chief of the King. He was also no doubt influenced by the fact that they were in a position to prevent Matilda from being crowned Queen at Westminster.

'They hold a leading place in the affairs of this country,' he explained smoothly, 'because their city is so important. We have sent messengers to them asking them to attend and have given them safe conduct. I feel certain that they will arrive not later than today, so I suggest that with your kind permission we should now adjourn this meeting until tomorrow.'

So far everything seemed to be going well for Matilda. If the bishops had not seemed over-anxious to have her as Queen, at least nobody had come out in opposition. The Londoners were a different matter. She might well feel some anxiety about the attitude they might adopt since they had been the first to accept Stephen as king, and he had given them favours in return. In addition, the city lay in a part of the country which had been under his control ever since, and his Queen with her army was near at hand in Kent.

When they did arrive – not, as expected on that day, but on the day following – their somewhat surly attitude was not encouraging. First of all, they claimed to have come from the 'commune' of London. This was a somewhat nebulous claim. In general, a town was able to claim to be a commune when the citizens had formed themselves into a single corporation and had been given recognition as such by the King or their overlord. It seems probable that in the case of the Londoners, Stephen had recognised their claim to be a commune. They had also made some sort of a claim to have the right to elect a King, but they did not raise this point at Winchester.

They said that they had not come for the sake of confrontation, but merely to request that their lord the King should be set free. There were also a number of barons, they said, who had become members of their commune some time before and also wished to press this demand. It was a matter on which there was very strong feeling indeed.

Bishop Henry made a reply on much the same lines as his speech the day before and he pointed out the impossibility of granting this request. It was not a right or proper thing, he maintained, that Londoners of all people, who held a very special

position in English society, should take the part of men who had
deserted their lord in war, whose advice had led the King to
dishonour Holy Church, and whose aim in favouring the Londoners was simply to get money out of them. Henry was speaking
presumably of William of Ypres, Waleran of Meulan and those
other supporters of Stephen who had fled at Lincoln, but had
now joined his Queen.

The Londoners do not seem to have made any immediate
reply to the Bishop's speech. It may be that they were hesitating
what to say. At all events, there must have been some kind of a
pause in the proceedings, for a man called Christian, a clerk of
Stephen's Queen, seized the opportunity to jump to his feet and
hold out a document to Bishop Henry. Henry took it and read it
in silence. Then he called out, 'at the top of his voice', that the
document had no validity and was not at all the kind of thing
which should be read out to so distinguished an assembly. Becoming still more angry, he said that apart from what was written in
the document itself, and that was disgraceful enough, the name of
a witness appeared on it which he knew all too well. It was the
name of a man who only the year before, in this very same
chapter-house, had used the most insulting and disrespectful
language to reverend bishops.

Henry seemed to have lost his head in flying off at this tangent,
and the clerk, refusing to be intimidated, took back the document
and proceeded to read it aloud himself. It turned out to be an
appeal from Stephen's Queen.

'I earnestly implore all the assembled clergy, and particularly
the Bishop of Winchester, the brother of my lord,' she had
written, 'that he will restore my lord to his throne since wicked
men, his own men who had sworn to be faithful to him against all
others, have cast him into bondage.'

Henry of Winchester, who had by now collected himself, gave
a reply to much the same effect as that he had given to the Londoners. They, meanwhile, had been having a discussion among
themselves and were a little more conciliatory. They said they
would take the Council's decision back with them to London,

put it before their fellow citizens and give it what backing they
could. They did not, however, give the impression of being
ready to offer an enthusiastic welcome to a new ruler.

The next day, Thursday, passed off uneventfully. Sentence of
excommunication was passed on a number of the King's party,
including William Martel, who had once been King Henry's
cupbearer and was now Stephen's steward. He had very much
annoyed Bishop Henry some time before by stealing and making
off with a number of his possessions. Finally the Bishop turned
his attention once more to Matilda and solemnly pronounced
that 'those who cursed her should be accursed themselves, and
those who blessed her were themselves blessed'. He then pronounced sentence of excommunication on those who opposed
her, and conferred absolution on those who obeyed her.

He had, in fact, kept his bargain and done his very best for
Matilda, but he cannot have felt entirely satisfied with the way
things had gone. The Londoners were quite clearly going to be
a problem, and if they remained hostile, it would be difficult, if
not impossible, for Matilda to be crowned in Westminster Abbey.

Her position, in fact, was still not very well assured, quite apart
from the worry over the coronation, for most of her support was
still drawn almost exclusively from the west and the south-west,
those areas which she had dominated since her landing. Many
of the leading barons had still made no move to recognise
her, and a large number of them were far more engrossed
in quarrelling amongst themselves than in deciding between
Stephen and Matilda. Fresh fuel was given to these quarrels by
Matilda herself, for she now began to take land away from one
and give it to another in a completely arbitrary manner. She
cancelled solemn contracts with royal abandon, and, continuing
to show her new haughtiness, gave grave offence to a number of
people. When supporters of Stephen came over to her side,
instead of welcoming them, she would often receive them
'coldly' and at times with outright hostility. Some she even drove
from her presence, calling insults and threats after them. She had
grounds, of course, for thinking them traitors and perjurers, but

it was a short-sighted way to behave. Worst of all, however, was the way she now began to treat her loyal brother Robert of Gloucester, to whom she owed so much, her uncle King David of Scotland, who at least had steadily acknowledged the validity of his vow to recognise her, and Henry of Winchester, not, of course, a man she could be expected to trust, but a man supremely important to her cause. They seem to have been in constant attendance on her at this time, travelling round in her company, but she soon began to take them for granted and to show them increasing disrespect.

When they came into her presence with some request or other, entering on bended knee and bowing to her, she did not rise respectfully as she should have done, but would call out a peremptory refusal. Sometimes she would not even listen to what they had to say. She was rude to them in public and paid no attention to the advice they gave her, advice worth having since it came from experienced and intelligent men, but went ahead and made decisions for herself, as the mood took her.

Some of this may be slanted and malicious reporting by writers who favoured Stephen, and it may be significant that William of Malmesbury, Robert of Gloucester's protégé, says nothing of this arrogant and ill-natured behaviour, while Gilbert Foliot, writing at a later date, remarks on her freedom from arrogance. All the same, there are too many reports of her 'haughty spirit' at this time for there not to be some foundation for them, and her actions make it clear that she was at the very least tactless.

She had early shown that she was not going to keep the promises she had made to Henry of Winchester that he should be in charge of church appointments. There was a dispute, for instance, over the bishopric of Durham, which her uncle, King David, wanted to give to his Chancellor William Cumin, while the cathedral chapter was anxious to assert their right to free canonical election. Henry of Winchester backed the chapter, but Matilda, ignoring everything he said, went ahead with arrangements to give the bishopric to William. She even proposed to invest him with the ring and staff herself, as soon as she was crowned, an act which would have alienated all the clergy and stirred up the old investiture dispute, with which she should certainly have been familiar since not only her father but her first husband the Emperor as well had been involved in endless difficulties over it.

In addition to opposing Henry over Church affairs, she also proceeded to snub him over a family matter concerning his nephew Eustace, Stephen's eldest son. His mother had brought Stephen the 'honour' of Boulogne at the time of their marriage, and in addition Henry I had made a gift to Stephen of the county of Mortain. Henry of Winchester thought it only right and just that these inheritances should be handed over to Eustace so long as his father was held captive, but Matilda gave him a curt refusal.

It was an act of incredible folly. There was nobody she should have been more anxious to attach to her party than Bishop Henry, and it was madness to offend him. And offended he was. He was so angry, in fact, that he left Matilda's court and kept away for a considerable time, in spite of repeated invitations to join her.

On the face of it, it seems unbelievable that an intelligent woman should have acted with such stupidity, and there is no really satisfactory explanation. She may have been a 'virago', William of Malmesbury's word, which meant no more than that she had masculine traits of character. She may have been stubborn; perhaps she was naturally imperious. She was, after all, a granddaughter of the 'stark' and formidable William the Conqueror, and had been the wife of an Emperor. If this was so, she had been able to control these tendencies in the past, and to make herself liked, very much so in Germany. She had behaved badly to Geoffrey of Anjou during her first year of marriage, but then the marriage was hateful to her. She may also have thought that she could establish a position of domination over a boy eleven years younger than herself. She was proved wrong, and she went back to him. After that, the marriage, though never happy, was kept going with reasonable success. In other words, she was sensible.

So why, at this time, was her behaviour so far from sensible? She knew the weaknesses of her position, she knew that Henry of Winchester's support was vital to her – she had shown that by her first overtures to him – and although she was now acknowledged as 'Domina' – 'Lady' – she was not yet Queen. She could not afford to take risks.

It has been suggested that she might have been experiencing an early menopause – she was thirty-nine – and that this may have unbalanced her judgement; but it does not seem very plausible. Not many women are seized with sheer folly at such times, after all.

Perhaps it is necessary to look back at the whole course of her life even to guess at an explanation. The chronicler Orderic Vitalis always remembered how he was sent across the sea from England to Normandy when he was ten years old 'unknown to all and knowing nobody'. Like Joseph, he recalled, 'I heard a language to which I was an utter stranger.' So did Matilda, and she was only eight. Orderic speaks of his 'bitter weeping'; if Matilda wept, there is no record of it, but it would be inconceivable if she did not, suddenly separated as she was from all that she had ever known.

She made a success of marriage to her sombre and sometimes cruel husband. She became a German through and through, only to be told that she must come back to England and turn herself into an Englishwoman again.

She had the splendid prospect of succession to the English throne dangled before her, but in the immediate present she was forced into marriage with a boy of fourteen – a boy, moreover, much below her in rank. Given that she would accept her father's right to dispose of her in marriage as he chose, she must still have been aware of the contrast between the glories of her past as Empress, the glories of her future prospects as Queen of England, and her immediate helplessness. It must have been very difficult to be a woman in the Middle Ages, enjoying considerable power and freedom in some ways, yet denied every vestige of independence in others. Matilda, in fact, fared worse than the ordinary gentlewoman of her time, for it was fairly common for a widow, even though her immediate overlord had the right to dispose of her in marriage as he chose, to be allowed to buy herself out of an unwelcome marriage, or even to purchase the right not to re-marry at all. Matilda was given no choice.

And now she was in a position of real power. She was to be Queen; she was to rule. It may well have been a temptation to make her power felt; but she seems to have lost her head altogether and behaved like the fool she was not.

Only a few more weeks remained to her before she lost – threw away – almost everything she had gained. She made Oxford her headquarters while the negotiations about her coronation were being carried out. The Londoners were being distinctly difficult, but Robert of Gloucester was doing his best for her by talking in a friendly way with the leading citizens, and in the end, terms were agreed; but it was only just before Midsummer Day, 24 June 1141, that she was at last able to enter the city.

It was a splendid city. The English were considered a cheerful and merry people at this time; their unquenchable gaiety, in fact, was often compared to the serious and sedate demeanour of the average Frenchman. 'Nowhere', wrote a monk of St Alban's, 'are faces more joyous at the board, or hosts more eager to please, or entertainments more sumptuous.'

And of all this gaiety and merriment, London was the very peak and centre. Not only was it famous for its power and its wealth, but it was 'cheerful in its sports'. There is a detailed description of it, written some thirty years later, but it was probably not very different at the time Matilda made her official entry as future Queen. The author of this description, William fitzStephen, a chaplain and biographer of Thomas Becket, writes of its noble churches, its famous Tower 'very great and strong' and the pleasant suburbs with their 'spacious and beautiful gardens, planted with trees'.

He describes the schools and the fame of their scholars, the great merchants and their trade, and the amenities of his city.

'There is in London, on the river bank, a public cookshop.

There daily you may find food according to the season, dishes of
meat, roast, fried and boiled, large and small fish, coarser meats
for the poor and more delicate for the rich, such as venison, and
big and small birds. If any of the citizens should unexpectedly
receive visitors, weary from their journey, who would prefer not
to wait until fresh food is brought and cooked, they hasten to
the river bank and there they find all they need ... Those of
sophisticated tastes do not have to go far in search of sturgeon or
any other delicacy ...'

Outside the city, on every sixth day of the week, there was a
sale of horses held on a large field. Earls, barons and many
citizens attended it, for it was 'pleasant to see the high-stepping
palfreys with their gleaming coats as they go through their paces'.
There were horses there of every kind: colts, sumpter-horses, and
above all war-horses, 'costly, elegant of form, noble of stature,
with ears quivering, necks raised, and sturdy haunches'.

Merchandise from all over the world was brought to London:
gold from Arabia, spices, incense, arms, precious stones, 'furs
and sables from Norway and Russia, and purple silk from China'.
And, of course, French wines. Although, says fitzStephen, the
citizens are well-conducted on the whole, London has two
plagues, 'the immoderate drinking of fools and the frequency of
fires'. Fires, of course, were a perpetual dread in those days of
timber-built houses.

There were sports, too, to be enjoyed. 'It is not fitting,' says
fitzStephen, 'that a city should be merely useful and serious-
minded, unless it is also pleasant and cheerful.' There were plays
to be seen of a sacred character, cock-fighting, ball games, and
every Sunday in Lent the young men would swarm out into the
fields on war-horses and stage mock battles. All through the
summer, on every feast day, there was archery, jumping, wrestling, and throwing the javelin. And dancing – 'Cythera leads the
dances of maidens, and until the moon rises, the earth is shaken
with flying feet.'

In the winter, there was skating. 'When the great marsh that
washes the north wall of the city is frozen over, the young men

go out in swarms to play games on it. So swift is their motion, that sometimes their feet slip and they fall on their faces. Others, more skilled in winter sports, put on their feet the shin-bones of animals, and holding poles in their hands with which they strike the ice, they are propelled swift as a bird in flight or a bolt shot from an engine of war . . . Often a leg or an arm may be broken . . . but youth is greedy of glory.'

A merry, busy city then, with plenty to do, trade thriving, fine buildings, great men; but smelly to a degree. All refuse and sewage was simply dumped in the narrow streets, which had a gulley in the middle down which the more liquid part of the refuse drained away. A few of the larger and richer houses had cesspits in their gardens, but that was the exception. The stench must have been appalling. None the less, by the standards of the day, London was a magnificent city and the Londoners, with their special privileges, a force in the land. Matilda could not do without their goodwill.

At first, the Londoners behaved correctly and received her with suitable displays of enthusiasm, in spite of their long hesitation. She was greeted with 'processional honours' at Westminster, and took up residence there, just outside the city gates, while preparations for her coronation in the Abbey went ahead. She was still behaving with 'intolerable arrogance' however, and she undid much of the good work her brother had done. It was about this time that she twice used the title 'Regina' – Queen – in issuing charters, and she had already embarked on the royal business of conferring honours, rewarding faithful followers and buying support from new ones. Among other gifts, she confirmed Geoffrey de Mandeville, the hereditary castellan of the Tower of London, as Earl of Essex. He had received this title from Stephen only a year or so before; but he was to become a notorious turncoat, pushing up the bidding for his allegiance with every shift in the balance of power.

Stephen's Queen sent envoys to Matilda in London imploring her to release her husband from his cruel captivity, and a number of nobles added their pleas to hers, affirming that if only he could be free, he would become a monk, or a pilgrim, but all they got from Matilda was a peremptory 'No'.

She then received a delegation of the citizens of London, who asked to be subject to the laws of King Edward instead of the harsher laws of her father the King, but Matilda was having none of that. On the contrary, she abruptly demanded a very large sum of money from them. Taken aback, they began to plead that their resources were very much reduced owing to the war, that they had spent a great deal in giving relief to the poor, who were on the very brink of famine, and that they had subsidised King Stephen so liberally that they were almost in penury themselves. So, with the greatest respect, they begged her, out of consideration for their distressed financial state, to levy only moderate taxes on them; and if a new tax must be imposed, at least to allow them time in paying it.

It was certainly tactless of the citizens to mention their generosity to Stephen, but it was worse than tactless, it was folly, for Matilda to treat them with hostility. She knew that they had only been persuaded with difficulty to receive her at Westminster – again not a fact to endear them to her, but a warning none the less that they must be treated with care. Yet all of a sudden, she seems to have been transported with fury. Glaring at them, frowning fiercely, every trace of the 'gentleness of her sex' wiped from her face, she burst out at them.

'Yes indeed,' she said, 'you have poured out money on the King. You have squandered your wealth in strengthening his cause. And weakening mine. Long have you plotted with my enemies to do me harm. You have no claim whatsoever to any leniency on my part nor any right to have your tax reduced in the slightest degree.'

What she said, of course, was entirely true; but she should never have said it, for the citizens left her presence greatly upset and seething with discontent. Stephen's Queen now saw that her opportunity had come. She had already assembled an army in Kent and she now marched it to London and drew it up on the south side of the river. From there she made forays into London,

burning, destroying and looting, and so creating further dis-
illusion on the part of the citizens, who by this time longed to be
rid of Matilda. They saw their city constantly under attack, and
they themselves had to take refuge in their houses 'like hedge-
hogs'. Nobody seemed ready to help them. Help, indeed, was
the last thing they could expect from Matilda, who gave all
the signs, they thought, of being a cruel and rapacious ruler. So
they decided they had made a mistake in recognising her, and
entered into negotiations with Stephen's party about the possibility of rescuing him and restoring him to the throne.

Matilda, apparently, had no inkling at all of what was going
on. She sent out to remind the citizens that they had still not paid
their tax, and on 24 June she sat down to a 'hot dinner' in her
lodgings at Westminster feeling perfectly secure. Suddenly all
the bells of London rang out. It was the call to arms. The citizens
came running out of the city gates, making towards Westminster
in a savage rush 'like bees out of a hive'. The Empress heard the
roar of voices and the wild howling of the mob just in time to
jump on a horse and ride for her life. There was no time to gather
up one single thing; all her possessions were left behind her.

It was nothing like an orderly retreat; it was a wild scramble
to escape. Everyone made for safety as best he could, not at first
heading for anywhere in particular, but simply making sure of
getting away. Almost as Matilda left, the citizens came pouring
in, pillaging, burning and destroying all that they found. Some
of the barons who had been with her at the start quickly forgot
all thought of their duty to protect their Queen and made off on
their own, riding up any by-way or lane in the hope that somehow or other they might reach the safety of their own lands.
Henry of Winchester, who may have had some knowledge of the
uprising in advance, disappeared somewhere on the way; Robert
of Gloucester did not. He stayed with Matilda, as also did her
uncle, David of Scotland, and a few of her other supporters from
among the barons. At last they reached the comparative safety
of Oxford.

It was a dramatic reversal of fortune and a severe setback to all

Matilda's hopes. Stephen's party, on the other hand, took new heart and began to make plans to set him free. His Queen, above all, made more strenuous efforts than ever to increase the size of her army and win as many new supporters as possible. Like her rival Matilda, she put aside all feminine weaknesses and set herself to play the part of a man. When pleading and prayers produced no effect, she made promises, she mortgaged her assets, she sold jewels and put herself into debt to help her husband. There was nothing she would not do for him. And after the flight of Matilda from London, she began to have much greater success, for the barons were soon flocking to what now looked like the winning side. William of Malmesbury dismissed these new recruits as only the young and frivolous from among the nobility, the sort of men who enjoyed a good exciting battle more than peace. The fact remains, however, that they were back on Stephen's side and fighting against Matilda. The versatile Geoffrey de Mandeville changed sides once more, almost certainly extracting even better terms than the last time.

The one really important asset that the Empress Matilda still held was Stephen. Up to this time, he had been treated reasonably well, but now Matilda gave orders that he should be put in chains attached to iron rings. According to William of Malmesbury, he had been found outside his quarters once or twice, particularly at night, when he had apparently either dodged or bribed his gaolers. That, at least, was the excuse; not that an excuse was needed, for confining prisoners in chains was nothing exceptional at the time. This new severity was probably a sign, however, of a new feeling of insecurity on Matilda's part.

She did not stay long in Oxford castle, strongly fortified though it was, but pushed on to her old strongholds in the West Country. She longed, perhaps, for the support and comfort of her faithful follower, Miles of Gloucester. She had depended on him for advice and help ever since she had landed in England, and according to Miles's own account, she had scarcely eaten one single meal since her arrival other than by his munificence and contrivance. She was naturally anxious to reward him for so much faithful service, and it was about this time that she created him Earl of Hereford.

Uncomfortable rumours began to reach Matilda that the loyalty of Henry of Winchester could by no means be taken for granted. He had apparently made no secret of his disillusionment with her and had been complaining to everybody who would listen that she had broken all her promises, and that while the barons kept their word, she did not. He said her behaviour had become altogether intolerable, and he even hinted that she was planning to seize him. Naturally Stephen's Queen heard of these complaints along with everybody else; and she had, in any case, been making efforts to win him back to his brother's side. They had a secret meeting at Guildford about this time, and influenced, so it was said, by her tears and promises, Henry agreed to do all that he could to set his brother free.

Robert of Gloucester set off for Winchester on the rather hopeless mission of putting affairs to rights and winning back the Bishop's loyalty. But he had been a shaky supporter from the start, and he was not likely to want to back a loser; and that was what Matilda looked like at the moment. Her cause, however, was not by any means hopeless. The situation could still be retrieved.

Henry of Winchester evidently thought not, and Robert went back to his sister, who was at Oxford, to report the failure of his mission. They had lost him. He had not come out against Matilda in so many words, but there could be little doubt of his intentions.

It is not known whether Matilda took time to reflect on how foolish she had been in alienating the Bishop and so many others. Outwardly, at least, she seemed to be entirely concentrated on the problems of the present, and she acted promptly. Hastily summoning her scattered followers to join her, she rode at the head of a 'vast army' to the city of Winchester.

9 Escape

Empress Matilda reached Winchester some time towards the end of July 1141 and was received into the city without any sign of open hostility. She took up residence in the royal castle and from there sent a message to the Bishop asking him to come to her. If he genuinely feared that she intended to arrest him – and his own brother had demonstrated that even a bishop could not count on the safety of the 'king's peace' – then this was obviously an invitation he would not be keen to accept. He sent back a somewhat ambiguous reply to the effect that he would 'prepare himself'. The preparations he in fact made consisted in sending out messages to all possible supporters asking them to join him, and then shutting himself up in his own castle of Wolvesey. Among the messages he sent out, there was one, naturally, to Stephen's queen, asking her for help. He also set about recruiting as many mercenary soldiers as he could find, for he was determined not to be made a prisoner, if he could help it.

A complex situation then developed. Matilda besieged the Bishop in his castle, and he responded by raining down firebrands on his own city of Winchester, which was soon in flames. According to William of Malmesbury, an 'entire nunnery' within the city walls was destroyed by fire as well as the monastery of Hyde just outside. Many churches were burnt as well; but it was the citizens of Winchester who suffered the worst. Their homes were burnt to ashes, flames encompassed them, they lost all that they possessed; many lost their lives. Soon, on top of everything else, there was a shortage of food in the town.

Stephen's Queen Matilda had lost no time in bringing up her army, now augmented by a strong force of Londoners, and the besiegers of the Bishop became the besieged in their turn. 'All England was there in arms.' Matilda's situation became increasingly precarious, for the opposing troops concentrated on preventing supplies from reaching her, and however well stocked a castle might be, the food, if not the water, was bound to run out sooner or later. The Queen's army had burnt the town of Andover, which was on the road to the north, so preventing supplies arriving from the direction of Gloucester and Bristol, the main centres of the Empress's party, and they were already in control of all the roads from the east.

A severe famine was threatening the citizens of Winchester, and in the castle the situation had become so serious that a rather desperate manœuvre was decided upon. A force was to be sent out from the castle to Wherwell, which lay on the river Test about nine miles to the north-west on the road to Andover. A garrison of three hundred men was to be established there and some fortifications quickly run up. By this means, it was hoped that the arrival of supplies into the city could be maintained and that it would also make a good centre from which to harass Stephen's army.

Either the plan was betrayed, or the movement of soldiers was observed, for a force from the Queen's army, under her most experienced general, William of Ypres, suddenly launched an attack on them when they were still on the outskirts of Wherwell, and defeated them decisively. The larger part of the force was either captured or killed, but some managed to take refuge in the nunnery at Wherwell. Turning the chapel into a sort of fortress, they put up a desperate resistance, until firebrands were thrown in on them, the building caught fire, and they were driven out, half-burnt, to surrender as they could.

'It was a horrifying and lamentable thing to see,' wrote a contemporary, 'soldiers in armour were trampling in warlike style over the pavement of the church, the house of worship, the house of prayer; in one part of this holy place, men were being done to death, in another prisoners were being dragged along the floor, bound with straps; here flames were leaping up and devouring the roof, there the holy nuns, driven from their cloister by fire, were running about, uttering cries of fear and lamentation as they went.'

The news of the disaster brought dismay to Matilda and her supporters in the castle. The siege had been going on for over six weeks by this time, their position had grown ever more desperate, and this defeat seemed the final blow. They were very much afraid that William of Ypres, encouraged by his success at Wherwell, might make some new attack on them which they were in no shape to resist. There seemed, in fact, to be nothing for it but retreat, and retreat under obviously hazardous conditions. There was no question of saving their possessions, for they must travel light. And so, with little more than their arms and what they stood up in, Matilda and her army rode out of the gates of Winchester on Sunday, 14 September in good military order.

The good military order and the planned retreat did not last long. They were immediately attacked by the opposing troops with such violence and in such numbers that they could not hold their ranks and were scattered in total disorder. Knights fled in every direction, throwing off their coats of mail as they went, flinging their shields and their arms behind them, anything to lighten the burden on their horses and enable them to gallop faster. It was panic. It was rout. Robert of Gloucester kept his head and his courage, and putting his sister in charge of Brian fitzCount, he sent them on in front, while he stayed in the rear to hold up the enemy as long as he could and give them a chance to escape.

It was a nightmare scene of chaos and destruction. 'Horses which had thrown their riders were galloping loose, while others, ridden to exhaustion, lay gasping out their life on the ground.' The ground itself was strewn with shields and coats of mail and weapons of every kind. There were costly robes, gold and silver cups, priceless ornaments scattered everywhere, while knights, and even barons, threw away their insignia of rank and fled ingloriously on foot. They had no thought but to get away. Some crept into hiding places, if they could find any, with the idea of lying up until they could see a chance to escape. Many were discovered, many murdered.

The King of Scots was captured three times over, but each time he managed to bribe his captors to let him go, until at last, 'exhausted and grief-stricken', he came to his own country. Robert of Gloucester was not so lucky. Fighting a gallant rearguard action, he came under attack by the Flemish mercenaries under William of Warenne and was taken prisoner, with all his men, while they were attempting to ford the river Test at Stockbridge.

Matilda got away. With Brian beside her, she rode at full gallop until they came to Ludgershall, a distance of twenty miles. They dared not stay there long, however, so they mounted again, Matilda now riding astride, 'in the male fashion' as a chronicler puts it, and struggled on for another eighteen miles to what should have been the security of Devizes castle. Even here they did not feel entirely safe, but Matilda was 'half dead' by this time with shock and fatigue and she could ride no further. So she was strapped to a litter between two horses, and thus, ignominiously, she reached at last the safe stronghold of Gloucester.

Here she was joined by Miles of Gloucester. He had thrown away his arms and his armour and he arrived quite alone, weary to death and half-naked. Brian fitzCount, of course, was already with her. 'Their mutual devotion, one to the other, had always been single-hearted,' wrote a contemporary, 'and now, in the hour of their greatest need and distress, they were not divided.'

Is he suggesting that Brian and the Empress were lovers? *Were* they lovers? There must have been some gossip about them or he would hardly have written in this way; but it is the only clue we have and it is unlikely that the truth will ever be known. Certainly Brian was constantly at her side, and Matilda was a beautiful woman still under forty. For her part, she may well have been attracted by Brian, who was an exceptional man in every way, and she had no love for her husband to restrain her; but it can only be a guess.

Matilda was later called a woman 'girt about with fortitude', and certainly at this crisis of her affairs she put aside all feminine weakness and showed an 'iron spirit unbroken by adversity'. She needed it for she had reached the very nadir of her fortunes, and so soon after she had been on the heights. Even Stephen, still her captive, was no longer the asset he had been, for her brother Robert, who had always been at the head of her affairs, was a prisoner, too, and it looked as though she might have to barter Stephen for Robert's freedom.

As for Robert, he was behaving, in adversity, with his usual impeccable honour and integrity. He was particularly admired, according to William of Malmesbury, for the fact that nobody ever saw him broken in spirit or depressed by his misfortunes. He was held prisoner at Rochester and was treated with kindness, for at first it was hoped that he might be persuaded to go over to Stephen's side. He was offered every possible inducement to do so by Stephen's Queen; he was even promised 'lordship over the whole land', and that he should be 'second only to the King'.

Robert steadily refused to consider any offers without the consent of his sister. 'I am not a free man,' he said. 'I am in the power of others. When I am once more my own master, then I will decide on what seems best with regard to your proposal. That is my answer.'

Efforts to arrange a straight exchange of Robert of Gloucester for Stephen had already been made, but Robert had firmly opposed this idea. He said that he was, after all, much inferior to the King in rank, and the exchange would only be fair if all the men captured with him were freed at the same time. Negotiations dragged on, with Robert's wife Mabel at least as anxious as the Queen to arrange terms. Threats to Robert from the Queen that if he remained intransigent he would be sent over to Boulogne and imprisoned there were countered by his threat that Stephen would, in that case, be sent over to the wilds of Ireland. It seemed stalemate.

The argument that in the end did produce an effect on Robert was the one brought forward by his own friends. They reminded him that the defeat at Winchester had been a major disaster and that Stephen's party might well follow this up by inflicting similar defeats on them in the future, perhaps picking them off one by one. They might even capture the Empress. It was of the first importance, therefore, that he should be free and able to manage her affairs again. So the original proposal of a straight exchange of Stephen for Robert was revived, and this time accepted, but only after an elaborate set of conditions had been worked out to make quite certain that neither side should cheat on the arrangements.

On 1 November 1141 Stephen was released from Bristol, leaving his Queen and his son and two nobles behind him as hostages; two days later, he met Robert, still a prisoner, at Winchester, where he made an unsuccessful attempt to win him over to his side. Next Robert was released, leaving his son William behind him as a hostage. When he reached Bristol, Stephen's Queen and son and the two nobles were released, and when they reached Winchester, Robert's son was set free; so bringing the whole complicated charade to an end. They were all back, more or less, where they had started after Matilda's landing two years before; and the kingdom continued to be 'torn to pieces with rapine, murder and sacrilege'.

Henry of Winchester found himself in an awkward position once more, for although he had now fought on Stephen's side and could claim to be a least partly responsible for his release, he was none the less faced with the task, as Legate, of bringing the Church back into formal allegiance to the King and explaining away, if he could, their so recent acceptance of Matilda. It was a challenge calling for all his resource.

He called a Council at Westminster on 7 December 1141. 'I cannot describe the proceedings of the Council quite so exactly and precisely as I described the earlier one,' wrote William of Malmesbury, 'as this time I was not there myself.' But he seems to have had very good sources.

First of all, Bishop Henry read out a letter he had received from the Pope some time before in which he rebuked the Legate, though in mild terms, for shirking the task of releasing his brother from captivity. He urged him to do all in his power to set Stephen free. It was a convenient alibi and excused a change of sides.

Now the King *was* free; indeed he was present at the Council and after entering the chamber, he proceeded to make a formal complaint that men who had sworn allegiance to him had taken him prisoner and by their treatment of him had come near to killing him. Yet he had never refused them justice.

Bishop Henry's moment of maximum difficulty had come. He had already made himself unpopular by his shifts and turns, and now he had to put a respectable face, somehow or other, on his latest change. He began by saying that in recognising Empress Matilda as Queen, he had acted under force majeure; he had never *wanted* to recognise her. But he had no choice; his brother, after all, had just suffered a disastrous defeat, his barons had either been put to flight or were sitting on the fence, waiting to see how things turned out, while the Empress, with 'all the sound and fury of arms', had surrounded Winchester. What was he to do? (He made no mention of their private meeting at Wherwell.) He did what seemed best, unavoidable, at the time; but as things had turned out, Matilda had broken all the pledges she had made about the rights of the Church, and he had it on very good authority that she and her followers had even made a plot against his life. But God, in his mercy, had so directed the course of events that her hopes had come to nothing, he himself had escaped the danger which had threatened him, and he had been able to free his brother from his bonds. So, with the help of God and the Apostles, they must all now concentrate on assisting the King in every way possible – a King blessed by the goodwill of his people and the approval of the Apostolic See. As for the followers of the Countess of Anjou, those enemies of peace, they must be sentenced to excommunication; excepting only the Countess herself.

The description of Empress Matilda as the Countess of Anjou

was pointed and significant; it was the one title which gave her bitter offence. She always described herself as 'Empress', 'Queen of the Romans', or the 'Daughter of King Henry'.

It was an amazing change of front on Bishop Henry's part, and only the least informed of his hearers can have taken his speech very seriously. It did not, in fact, go down very well; it would have been astonishing if it had, but nobody spoke against him. All the clergy, according to William of Malmesbury, kept quiet either out of fear, or out of respect for the Papal Legate. The Empress, however, had sent an envoy to the Council, and he now spoke on her behalf. He forbade the Legate to make any decisions to her detriment, reminding him of a promise he had made her to give no aid to his brother, beyond perhaps supplying him with twenty knights at the most. She had come to England, he said, as a result of the many letters the Bishop had written to her, begging her to do so, and the King's capture and imprisonment had been chiefly due to his help and support.

This startling statement, if true, throws an interesting light on some of the Bishop's activities immediately after Matilda's landing.

Matilda's envoy spoke, apparently, in a very blunt and forthright manner without making the slightest attempt to flatter or win over Bishop Henry. He, on his side, as an experienced diplomat, had made up his mind that nothing would make him lose his temper or deflect him from his new path.

It was not a very successful occasion, but it achieved what it had set out to do, and it ended up with solemn sentences of excommunication being pronounced on all enemies of the Church; but William of Malmesbury, for one, was filled with pessimism about the future. England, he said, would once more fall into misery, and in misery it would remain, unless by the operation of God's mercy.

It was probably late in the following year, 1142, that Henry of Winchester, perhaps made uncomfortable by the presence of other people less adaptable in changing sides than himself, made an attempt to win over Brian fitzCount to Stephen's party. A number of letters seem to have passed between them, but only a fragment of a letter from the Bishop and one complete letter from Brian remain.

Henry of Winchester began his letter by reminding Brian of Lot's wife, who looked behind her and was turned into a pillar of salt. While Brian is looking back, he says, he fails to avoid a 'cause of offence' which is right under his eyes. He had apparently asked Brian to give an undertaking that his men would not interfere with travellers to the Bishop's fair of St Giles, and Brian had 'not refused'. Yet his own possessions had been seized and Brian's men had created disturbances both on the Bishop's land and on the roads leading into Winchester. It seemed, therefore, that he could no longer trust Brian and his men. He would have to number Brian among the 'faithless' of England . . .

Here, maddeningly, the letter breaks off. Brian makes it clear in his reply, however, that he is stung to fury that the turncoat Bishop, of all people, should dare to talk to him of broken promises. The letter reads as completely spontaneous, written in the passion of the moment, yet Brian is collected enough to marshal his case against the Bishop with great effect.

'To Henry, nephew of Henry the King.' Throughout the letter Brian underlines Henry's relationship to the late King, because by so doing he underlines his desertion of the King's daughter. 'You raise the story of Lot and his wife,' he writes. 'Well, I never saw them, or knew them, or knew their city – we were not living at the same time. But I have heard that it was an angel who ordered them to leave the city where they lived and not to look back. No one has ever told me not to look back. On the contrary, it is my duty to look back to the commands of Holy Church so that by bearing them ever in mind, I may avoid transgression.

'Now you yourself, a priest of Holy Church, enjoined me to be faithful to the daughter of your uncle King Henry, to help her to win her rights which had been taken from her by force and to hold on to all she already had . . . I look back to this command of yours and I am not afraid that I have committed some offence.

On the contrary, I have been obeying the orders of Holy Church.

'King Henry gave me land, but it has been taken from me – because I obeyed your command. In these times of great need, I am not reaping one acre of corn from all the lands the King gave me. Is it any wonder, then, if I take from others what I need to keep me and my men alive ... I should have no need to take the goods of other people, so that I may carry out your commands, if my own lands had been left me. You should know that neither I, nor my men, do this for money, or fief, or lands, either promised or given, but we do it solely out of obedience to your command, and out of regard for what is right.'

Over and over again Brian stresses the fact that it was the Bishop who had 'ordered' him to give Matilda his support, and what is the Bishop doing now? Here Brian makes a contemptuous reference to the Bishop's complaints about his fair. He had, he says, made no promise, but even so, if the Bishop had sent him particulars of his losses, he would have made them good. As for saying that he, Brian, should be numbered among the 'faithless' of England, all he has done is to strive to carry out the Bishop's orders. Rather should he be numbered among the faithful. He ends with a resounding challenge.

'Therefore let all the faithful of Holy Church know that I, Brian fitzCount, whom good King Henry brought up, who received from him arms and honour, am ready to prove either by battle or ordeal all these things of which I accuse Henry, Bishop of Winchester, nephew of King Henry and Legate of the Apostolic See.'

Brian fitzCount is one of the few men who were completely disinterested throughout these miserable years. He was not 'up for sale', like Geoffrey de Mandeville, he could not be bribed, he did not change with the changing winds of fortune like the slippery Henry of Winchester. On the contrary, he continued to hold the savagely isolated fortress of Wallingford for Matilda, far out on their eastern flank, and he fought on through everything. And in the end, he lost everything, for the sake of gratitude

E

to King Henry, for the sake of honour, and perhaps also for love of Matilda.

Events moved slowly after Stephen's release. Both sides seemed, for the moment, exhausted. Stephen's Christmas court was held that year in Canterbury, perhaps to mark his gratitude for the steady loyalty of the men of Kent, and he was crowned a second time on Christmas Day; but the ceremony of anointing was not repeated. His Queen was beside him, wearing a golden crown. It was some time during this period that he granted a charter to the ever versatile Geoffrey de Mandeville, which was probably a confirmation of the charter by which the Queen had bought back his support when Stephen was a prisoner.

Stephen went north to Yorkshire in the New Year and he visited the city of York, probably some time after Easter. He seems to have wanted to put a stop to a projected tournament between the Earl of York and Alan of Richmond, for these tournaments often turned out to be very bloody affairs and they were never popular with kings. Another object in going to Yorkshire was to raise an army, for he longed above all things to avenge the defeat of Lincoln and all the humiliations of captivity. He was successful in recruiting a fair number of supporters, but on the way south he became seriously ill – so ill, in fact, that a rumour spread abroad that he was dead.

Matilda seems to have spent the first few months after Stephen's release very quietly. She may have been trying to regain some measure of equilibrium after all that she had been through within less than a year; first the dizzying triumph at Lincoln, then her brief lease of power, and after that the disasters which had followed so quickly one upon another. The fear of capture must have been intense during her flight from London, and again from Winchester. If she had been taken, she would have had to face imprisonment for years, quite possibly for life. She might have been put in chains; she had, after all, put Stephen in chains. And even if her conditions of imprisonment had been merciful, she would have been parted, perhaps for ever, from her much-loved son Henry. Now she was safe, but there was no good news to give her courage; far from it. There was the bitter remembrance that she had been forced to give up Stephen, her most valuable asset.

Yet she never seems to have thought of giving up the struggle. It may be that some of her tenacity was rooted in her love of her son and her determination that he should have the throne of England after her.

At some time during this period, probably in early April 1142, she moved her headquarters to Oxford, and from there she went to Devizes for a meeting with Robert of Gloucester, who came over from Bristol. They were forced to come to what must have been a very unpalatable decision for Matilda: they decided to appeal to her husband Geoffrey of Anjou to come and help her.

So far as is known, Geoffrey had taken virtually no interest in Matilda's English adventure from the start. With his hereditary hatred of the Normans and his natural interest in events on the Continent, he had been concentrating on getting control of the Duchy of Normandy. And he had been making steady, if unspectacular, progress. He had besieged and captured two or three castles in 1140, and in 1141 he had been quick to take advantage of Matilda's successes in England by advancing into Normandy and sending messages to the leading barons demanding that they should surrender their castles into his hands. They, alarmed by the news from England, held a hasty conference, probably early in March, as a result of which Hugh, Archbishop of Rouen, accompanied by some of the leading magnates, went on a mission to Stephen's brother, Theobald of Blois. Once more they offered him the Duchy of Normandy and the English throne. Prudent man that he was, he found himself not at all attracted by the idea of taking on these 'vast cares'. He said he was prepared, however, given certain conditions, to hand over his rights, such as they were, to Geoffrey of Anjou. He does seem to have been a man of very modest ambition for all he asked for himself in return was the city of Tours and the release of Stephen. On the other hand, of course, Theobald had not very much to concede in the way of rights. It was one thing for a few of the Norman barons to offer him Normandy and the English throne, quite another to get possession of them.

Nothing seems to have come of these negotiations, but more significantly, perhaps, Waleran of Meulan, Stephen's steady supporter until now, came to terms with Geoffrey and handed over a castle which had belonged to him since the death of Henry I. It illustrates the fact that barons like Waleran, whose chief possessions lay in Normandy, were more concerned with protecting their own position there than in worrying over what might happen to Stephen.

Geoffrey next gained possession of Lisieux, which had been holding out against him for some time, as well as the important stronghold of Falaise. In addition, all the lands in the neighbourhood of Rouen surrendered to him, but not Rouen itself. He was, therefore, in a far stronger position than when Matilda had sailed for England two years before, and he owed his successes in large part to Robert's victory at the battle of Lincoln.

After the meeting between Matilda and Robert of Gloucester at Devizes in April 1142, envoys were sent to Geoffrey formally inviting him to come to England and help his wife to win her inheritance there. His reply came before they held their next meeting early in June, which was probably held chiefly to discuss what he had said. It was not precisely what they had wanted. There were some flattering references to Robert of Gloucester; Geoffrey had long known of his sound judgement, his loyalty and unflagging energy. Unfortunately, however, the envoys sent over to him had been men of whom he knew nothing at all. Now, if the Earl himself would come, they could discuss the whole affair in detail and he would do his very best to meet the Earl's wishes. If Earl Robert was not prepared to come, however, it would be sheer waste of time to send anybody else.

Some of Matilda's supporters thought Geoffrey's offer worth pursuing, and they combined in trying to persuade Robert to undertake the mission. He was far from enthusiastic. In fact, at first he refused absolutely. The journey was difficult and dangerous, he said, and he would have to make his way through enemies on both sides of the Channel. He was worried about his sister's safety as well. He did not feel he could trust anybody else to look after her while he was away; after all, they had been not far from deserting her at the time when he had been a captive. However, he gave in at last; but he did prove how genuine was his anxiety for Matilda by demanding hostages from the leading nobles to take with him to Normandy.

This was agreed, and off he went, making for Wareham, which was then in the hands of his eldest son William. He sailed in June, but encountered a freak summer storm when he was in the middle of the Channel. All his ships but two were scattered by the violence of the wind, but Robert himself came safely to port, and immediately sent messengers to Geoffrey asking him to meet him at Caen.

The meeting was *not* satisfactory. On the surface, Geoffrey was charm itself and only too ready to help, but alas, he had his own troubles, as he pointed out at some length. Very *many* troubles. For one thing, there were a number of castles in the hands of rebels and he could not go off to England without reducing them first. Robert was far from pleased at the delay, but in order to deprive Geoffrey of any excuse for not coming, he offered to join him in taking the castles. They took ten; but it was still not the end, for Geoffrey then devised fresh excuses for putting off the journey. Altogether he kept Robert in Normandy helping him, instead of setting off himself to aid his wife, for not far off six months. By then news had begun to reach Robert that his sister was in danger, and he refused to wait one moment longer. Geoffrey still said that it was really not possible for him to leave Normandy, but having made the most of Robert's help, he did make the concession, as a very great favour, of allowing his eldest son to accompany Robert to England. Henry was not quite ten years old, so could hardly be expected to fight, but he would be a valuable figurehead.

Before Robert had left England, he had taken the precaution of strengthening the defences of Oxford castle, making it as nearly impregnable as possible against all dangers except fire.

Matilda had established herself there after he was gone, and had busied herself with building a chain of forts to protect her communications with the West Country.

By the middle of June, Stephen had recovered from his illness; more than recovered, in fact, for he seemed inspired with new energy and vigour. 'He had awoken as one out of sleep.' He made a dash for Wareham, and the garrison, taken by surprise, hardly put up any resistance at all. The town was sacked and the castle fell into his hands. This was a brilliant stroke, for it deprived Robert of Gloucester of the port by which he had hoped to return. Stephen went from there to Cirencester, where the defenders, equally taken by surprise, were unable to hold the castle, which Stephen then burnt; likewise Radcot, Bampton and Matilda's other defence posts. Having thus isolated the Empress, he turned on Oxford itself and arrived there on 26 September.

Oxford castle, by its position, dominated the Thames valley, with its great waterway to the West Country, and it also commanded the main route south from Northampton to Winchester. To capture it would be a triumph; to capture it with Matilda inside might well bring the whole war to an end.

Stephen arrived at the ford from which Oxford takes its name, the old ford of St Frideswide to the south of the city. There had been a great deal of rain that summer, the waters were swollen and the ford was in flood. In a strange repetition of Robert's heroic assault on Lincoln, Stephen plunged into the water at the head of his men, and under a shower of arrows from the defenders he half swam, half waded across. Flinging themselves up the bank, they charged the enemy forces and drove them back inside the city walls in a rush. The usual slaughter and rapine followed, for Stephen's men killed as they went, and finally set fire to the city itself. Smoke and flames roared up on every side, and the few who escaped fled to take refuge in the castle. Matilda, on the battlements, must have watched the whole desperate action; and she knew that she must now face a long, and perhaps hopeless siege.

It *was* a long siege. For three months Stephen blockaded the castle, guarding carefully every avenue of approach so that no supplies, no morsel of food, could reach the beleaguered garrison. He was determined to capture Matilda; no hope of gain, he said, no fear of loss should deflect him from that one overriding purpose.

Robert, meanwhile, had made for Wareham, in spite of the fact that it lay in the power of the enemy, and he landed there after a particularly smooth crossing. All his fifty-two vessels came safely to land, together with two more that he had captured on the way. Although the castle was manned by picked knights, Robert, using powerful siege engines, assaulted it so energetically that the garrison asked for a truce while they sent a message to the King begging him for help. If it did not arrive, they were to surrender on an agreed date. This arrangement suited Robert very well for his chief aim was to lure Stephen away from besieging Matilda in Oxford. But Stephen held firm to his resolve – nothing should distract him from the siege – so the castle of Wareham was surrendered to Robert.

He went on to capture a castle at Portland and another at Lulworth near Corfe castle, and then summoned the Empress's supporters to meet him at Cirencester. They gathered all their forces there and began to make preparations to march on Oxford and rescue Matilda, even though they would be greatly outnumbered and their chance of success was slight.

Matilda and her men, meanwhile, after nearly three months of siege, had come almost to the end of endurance. Their supplies were exhausted, they were suffering agonies of hunger, and there seemed no prospect of relief. Outside lay Stephen and his army with over a thousand knights, closely investing the castle and battering it ceaselessly with stone-throwers and siege engines. The end was very near.

So a desperate escape was planned. It was near Christmas and the weather was bitterly cold; so cold, in fact, that the river was frozen over and all the land around lay under a covering of snow. Matilda, it was decided, would break out of the castle. Clothed from head to foot in white, so as to be less conspicuous against the snow, she was let down by a rope over the stark walls of the tower on the side which faced the river. With only three companions, she stole over the ice and through the enemy lines. Men were bivouacking round her, trumpets were sounding, she could hear the shouts of the guard. At any moment, she might be recognised and seized. But nobody saw her, except, it was said, for one man only, who may have been bribed, or who may have secretly favoured her cause. At all events, he kept silence.

On foot, she and her three companions struggled on over the frozen ground, stumbling and slipping and pushing their way through snow drifts, until at last they reached Abingdon, a good six miles away. There horses were waiting for them, and they rode on a further nine miles to Wallingford, the safe stronghold of Brian fitzCount. Stephen had lost his prize.

The news reached Robert of Gloucester and his army when they had already left Cirencester and were on their way to Oxford, so they changed their plans and made for Wallingford. 'And when the Empress saw her brother and her first-born son, she was glad beyond measure and held her earlier griefs and labours as nothing.'

Stephen's state of mind must have been very different. There is no record of what he said when he discovered that Matilda had escaped and that all the weary months of siege had been for nothing, but it is not difficult to imagine what he must have felt. The end of the war had seemed in sight, the capture of his rival at hand. Now all was to be done again. He did get possession of Oxford castle, however, and that was something. He accepted the terms of surrender offered by Matilda's men and allowed them to go free, putting a garrison of his own in their place.

And then, writes William of Malmesbury, in almost the last words of his *Modern History*, Matilda suggested to her followers that as it was Christmas, they should all give up fighting for the time being and go away home.

10 Disorder and Disarray≈◄

The war began its weary way again with the New Year of 1143.
Stephen marched at the head of a large body of troops to Wareham, but the castle was strongly defended and he evidently did
not think it worth a long siege. He contented himself with burning and pillaging the surrounding countryside and then made
north again to Wilton, near Salisbury. He seems to have intended
to strengthen the castle there, establish a strong garrison in it
and so provide himself with a base for further advances into the
West Country, the power base of the Empress. The Bishop of
Winchester, half-soldier, half-monk, as he has been called, joined
Stephen on the expedition and formed part of an advance party
led by the King. Winchester was not far away, about twenty-five
miles or so, and they were expecting the main army to move up
from there to join them.

Robert of Gloucester was too quick for them. He got word
of Stephen's movements, summoned his supporters and marched
on Wilton. There he drew up his army in three main divisions
and launched a violent attack on Stephen and his comparatively
small force. There was a short but fiercely fought battle, and
Stephen got the worst of it. He took flight, accompanied by his
brother the Bishop, while William Martel, the King's steward,
stood his ground, and fighting a determined rearguard action
managed to win enough time for the King to get clear away
before he himself was captured.

The battle became a rout, and Robert's men behaved after the
manner of all victorious armies of the time. They looted and

killed and set Wilton ablaze. They pursued their victims into the churches in which they had sought sanctuary and dragged them from the very altars with drawn swords. They burst open the gates of the convent of St Etheldreda and made captive all those who had taken refuge inside. They filled Wilton with 'tears and blood'.

Stephen was very sensitive about the fact that he had run away and deserted his men, for he could never forget the ill-fame which had darkened his father's life after abandoning his fellow Crusaders before Antioch. In consequence, he felt it imperative to ransom William Martel, whom Robert was holding prisoner at Bristol. The terms Robert demanded were very high indeed, no less than the surrender of Sherborne castle and all the land attaching to it. It was a price, however, which Stephen felt he must pay.

The Earl of Gloucester was very encouraged by his success and he and his men stayed on the attack. They took a whole series of castles, at the same time building up their own defences, or rather, forcing the local inhabitants to do it for them in a form of forced labour which was very unpopular and caused a good deal of resentment. There was very little actual fighting going on at this time, however, but it was only a 'shadow of peace', not true peace.

Matilda's son Henry was living in Bristol, where Earl Robert, who was a highly educated man himself, was supervising his education. A 'Master Matthew' had been put in charge of the boy's lessons, which he shared with his cousin Roger, one of Earl Robert's younger sons. Matthew was to instruct Henry in letters and in the 'good manners' suitable to his station in life, but there is no record of what else he may have been taught. He would almost certainly have learnt a little Latin and he probably picked up some English. He had a gift for languages and was later said to have some knowledge of every tongue from the 'French sea to the Jordan'. He may also have studied the usual subjects taught to boys at this time: grammar, rhetoric, and dialectic, and perhaps some arithmetic, geometry and astronomy. It is not

certain whether Matilda was with him, as she would surely have
wanted to be after their long separation, but she may have had to
spend most of her time at Gloucester, which had become her
headquarters.

It had been a dark time for Matilda, in spite of the victory at
Wilton; but Stephen now began to make mistakes – perhaps they
were unavoidable. He had saddled himself, at the cost of vast
concessions, with the dubious support of Geoffrey de Mandeville,
an ally whom he could scarcely be expected to trust, quite apart
from the fact that he had a long-standing grudge against Geoffrey.
When Stephen had gone north to fight at Lincoln, he had left his
Queen and his son's future wife, Constance of France, in the care
of Geoffrey de Mandeville. As castellan of the Tower of London,
he had seemed the most suitable person. After Stephen's defeat,
however, when the Queen decided to retreat into Kent, Geoffrey
would not let her take Constance with her, but kept her in the
Tower. The Queen had not allowed this insult to prevent her
from making handsome concessions to Geoffrey in order to win
him back to Stephen's side, and Stephen, when he came out of
captivity, had also been careful to conceal his resentment; but in
reality, he was waiting for an opportunity to have his revenge.

He waited two years; and during these two years, Geoffrey de
Mandeville grew ever more powerful, so that fear about what he
might be plotting was added to the King's desire for revenge.
This fear was fanned by some of his advisers, who kept telling
him that Geoffrey was a traitor, an enemy, a would-be destroyer.
It may have been true. Henry of Huntingdon says quite categorically that if Stephen had not taken action when he did, he would
have lost his crown. Even so, he hesitated a long time; but in the
end, he did act.

The whole affair was strangely reminiscent of the seizure of
the bishops at Oxford. Geoffrey de Mandeville was attending the
King's court at St Alban's in the autumn of 1143 when some
sort of fracas broke out, whether spontaneous or planned is not
certain, between him and the other barons. It was quite a violent
affair while it lasted, and the King intervened, supposedly to

restore order; but while he was attempting to do so, some of the barons came forward and accused Geoffrey to his face of plotting against the King. Geoffrey then infuriated them further by making no attempt to take the charge seriously and laughing it away. At this, the King and his barons arrested him.

Although there was no question of sacrilege this time, as there had been when the bishops were seized, the arrest of Geoffrey caused very nearly as much shock and disapproval as the affair at Oxford. It was an outrage against the accepted laws of hospitality of the time. The historian, William of Newburgh, said that it was 'ill-done' and that the King had obviously been more concerned with expediency than with honourable behaviour and Henry of Huntingdon took much the same line, calling it an action born of necessity rather than good faith. And even though Geoffrey himself was a layman, Stephen was still exposed to charges of outraging the rights of sanctuary, for the struggle had taken place on Church grounds and at one point the St Alban's knights had had to take up arms to defend the privileges of the Abbey. One circumstance that made it worse still was the fact that only a few months before, the King had attended a Council in London at which the freedoms of the Church had been re-asserted, and in particular the right of sanctuary.

Once Geoffrey had been arrested, there was only one course of action which Stephen could reasonably follow. Geoffrey was told that he must either surrender his castles or face execution. Geoffrey chose life. He was then taken to London, where he was forced to give orders personally to his garrison at the Tower, telling them to hand it over to the King. Geoffrey must have found this particularly hard, for his father had been castellan of the Tower before him and he had spent a good deal himself on strengthening it and making improvements. It was his main seat of power and it gave him, in effect, control of London. In addition, his ancestral lands in Essex and two castles (Saffron Walden and Pleshey) near Chelmsford were demanded of him. When these were surrendered, he was allowed to go free.

It was like the release of a mad dog. In his rage and his humili-

ation, he went storming through his lands in Essex, now taken
from him, and collected his followers together. He then went on
to the fenlands and there he recruited, without much difficulty, a
motley army of misfits and misdoers. With these men at his back,
he made a handsome living, plundering and stealing wherever he
went. He stormed the city of Cambridge, a rich prize, particularly
as he had no scruples about breaking into the churches, where
the citizens had stored their treasures. He then set the city ablaze
and left it to burn.

Feeling the need for some secure headquarters, he led his men
to Ramsey Abbey, which lay twenty miles to the north-west. It
stood on an island at this time, with only one approach to it, and
that over a narrow causeway, so that it was easily defended. He
arrived at daybreak when the monks were still asleep, hauled
them out of their beds and drove them out of doors, leaving them
no time even to dress. He then took over the Abbey and turned
it into a castle, stabling his horses in the cloisters and distributing
its manors and lands among his supporters by way of reward.

With Ramsey Abbey as his base, he launched on a career of
terror and violence, the echoes of which still come down to us
over the centuries in the shocked syllables of the chroniclers. He
seems to have been in the grip of a madness of revenge not only
against Stephen but against the world. The houses of religion
were his favourite prey, since they were full of rich treasure, but
even the smallest village church would yield him *something*; even
the ordinary countryman had some small possession worth taking.

His men, disguised as beggars, would knock on the doors of
cottages and discover what poor little hoard of wealth might be
inside. Then the owner would be seized at dead of night, dragged
away and tortured until a ransom was paid for his release. Sometimes it took every penny a man possessed to win back his freedom,
and sometimes he could only raise the money by mortgaging his
lands. These transactions occasionally appear in legal documents
of a later date. Godebald of Writtle, for instance, 'captured by
Count Geoffrey', mortgaged his land at Boreham 'for ransom to
be paid to the said Count' in the 'days of King Stephen'; the dry

record of a transaction of anguish. In those days, it was said, shall 'men desire to die, and death shall elude them'.

The Abbot of Ramsey, a brave man indeed, 'filled with the Holy Spirit', stalked fearlessly into Geoffrey's stronghold one day, and though menaced with swords, he seized up a firebrand and began setting fire to the tents. But neither fire, nor the sentences of excommunication which he hurled at them, could persuade these hardened sinners to leave. It was only astonishing that the Abbot was allowed to leave himself, still alive. It was said, however, that the Abbey buildings themselves reacted to the outrages inflicted on them, for the walls now began to drip with blood. The story was widely believed at the time and Henry of Huntingdon gives it an uncompromising endorsement. 'Many have seen it,' he wrote. 'I have seen it myself with my own eyes.'

The chronicler of nearby Peterborough has left a horrifying description of the state of England at the time.

'Every powerful man made castles for himself,' he wrote. 'They filled the land full of castles ... They greatly oppressed the wretched men of the land, for in the castles were devils and evil men. If they thought a man had wealth or treasure, they seized him – women as well as men. They seized them by night or by day, they flung them into prison for their gold and their silver, and tortured them with unspeakable torments. There were never martyrs so tormented as they. They hung them up by the feet, or by the thumbs, or by the head, loading their feet with heavy weights. They tied pieces of cord with knots in them round their heads, and twisted and turned them until they bit into the brain. They shut them up in dungeons with adders, and snakes, and toads; and so they killed them. Some they put in a "crucet house" – that is, in a chest, short, narrow and shallow. They put sharp stones in it first, and by pressing a man hard down into it, they broke his bones. In many of the castles were instruments of torture which were obscene and very dreadful ... Many thousands they starved until they were dead. I neither can, nor may, tell all the wounds nor all the sufferings which were inflicted on the unhappy men of this land. This went on for all the nineteen years that Stephen was king; and always things grew worse, and ever worse.

'From time to time, they would lay a levy on the towns which they called a "tenserie", and when the townsmen had nothing more to give, then they plundered and burnt the town. You might easily go a whole day's journey and never find one man in a town, nor the ground tilled. Then was corn dear, and meat, and cheese, and butter; for there was none in the land. Men died wretchedly of hunger, and some who had once been rich were forced to beg. Never has there been worse misery in the land, and no heathens ever did worse than those men did, for soon they spared neither church nor churchyard, neither bishop's land nor priest's, but everyone plundered another if he could. If two or three men came riding into a town, the men of the town would run away, for they would think they were robbers. The bishops and the clergy were forever laying curses on these men, but little did they care, for they were all accursed, and foresworn, and lost . . . Men said openly that Christ slept, and his saints.'

There were some parts of England which fared worse than others, of course, but the terror and the suffering were widespread, and it was worst of all in the lands ravaged by Geoffrey de Mandeville. Stephen had to do *something*, so he collected an army and marched north to try to confront Geoffrey, but Geoffrey had no intention of being confronted. The last thing he wanted was a pitched battle, and he somehow always managed to slip away with his men. In the end, Stephen had to content himself with putting up strong points in strategic places to box him in. One of these castles was at Burwell to the north-east of Cambridge, and it caused Geoffrey some annoyance as it threatened his lines of communications. Accordingly, in August 1144, he decided to attack it, but only after first making a careful reconnaissance to see if he could find a weak point. While he was riding round it, he was foolish enough to take off his helmet and loosen his coat of mail, as it was a very hot day. An ordinary archer, a man of the people, saw his opportunity and took it. He drew his bow, shot an arrow at Geoffrey and struck him on the head.

At first, Geoffrey made light of the wound, but in those days any wound was liable to become infected. He got as far as Mildenhall in Suffolk, but there he became seriously ill, and there he died. It was said that he repented of his sins at the last, but even so he died excommunicate. None could lift the sentence from him, whatever he might do, for Henry of Winchester had decreed that anyone who laid violent hands on the 'Lord's anointed' could only be absolved by the Pope.

Some Knights Templar came to Mildenhall as Geoffrey lay dying, and they threw over him the cloak of their order with its red cross. When he was dead, they carried his body with them to London, but they could not bury him, for no man who died excommunicate was allowed to be buried. So they enclosed his body in a leaden coffin and hung it in the branches of an apple tree so that it might not contaminate the ground.

Before he died, Geoffrey had at least done something to atone for his sins, for he left instructions to his son to restore Ramsey Abbey to its Abbot. It was a desolate inheritance: no more than a shell, the buildings ravished, the land untilled. There was nothing left inside, not so much as a 'pot to boil a cabbage stalk'. But the Abbot gathered his scattered monks together and they set about the task of restoring their Abbey to its former glory.

Geoffrey was the epitome of the 'bold, bad baron', and his story illustrates, in extreme form, the misery of England as the contenders for the crown still fought for the ascendancy. His dramatic fall from the heights of power had a great effect on the men of his day, for he had seemed invincible, as great as, or even greater than the King.

His death strengthened Stephen's position considerably as the most powerful of the barons was now out of his way. Matilda, on the other hand, may have lost a potential ally in Geoffrey, for there is some evidence that they had been plotting to engineer a major rising in East Anglia. But his loss was nothing compared to the blow she had already suffered by the death of Miles of Gloucester, her old and faithful friend, one of the three men who had steadily supported her in good times and in bad. He was killed in a hunting accident on Christmas Eve 1143. He was in the forest in pursuit of deer when one of his men took a careless shot at a stag and his arrow hit Miles in the chest.

He, like Geoffrey de Mandeville, died excommunicate. He had been hard put to it to find the means to pay the large army he had raised in Matilda's cause, and he had recourse to laying taxes on all the churches in his lands. He had also demanded that the Bishop of Hereford himself should pay the tax. The Bishop refused. He said that Church property, donated by devout believers for the service of God, should not fall into the hands of any layman; and if any layman attempted to seize it, he was as guilty of sacrilege as if he had snatched it from the altar.

Miles, desperate for money, sent his men to seize the Bishop's treasure and lay waste his land, but the Bishop, a man of spirit, retaliated by summoning his clergy and in their presence he laid the terrible sentence of excommunication on Miles. Terrible it was in the eyes of twelfth-century Christians, and terrible it seems to us today that a man of God should think it right to consign a soul to everlasting damnation as a punishment for the theft of material possessions. He also laid all Miles's lands under interdict so that none of the offices of the Church could be performed in them. Among other things, no man's body could be buried in the ground, cast into water or consumed by fire. It had to be left lying in the place, wherever it was, that the man had died; nobody must presume to move it until the author of the sacrilege had done due penance and restored to the Church all that he had taken, to the last farthing.

Miles, driven into a corner, promised to make full restitution, but it was a slow and complicated process, and it was still incomplete when death took him. Matilda must have missed him greatly for he, above all others, had cared for her and sheltered her, and it was in his castle of Gloucester that she had spent more time than anywhere else in England. The fact that he had died excommunicate must also have weighed on her conscience, for she must have realised very well that it had been for her sake that he had impoverished himself.

Throughout the years of 1144 and 1145 there was a constant crop of rebellions and desertions, siege and counter-siege, marches and withdrawals, all leading to little practical result. In 1145 Philip, a younger son of Robert of Gloucester, who had been put in charge of Cricklade castle, asked his father to help him by putting up some more castles in the district so as to hem in the King's forces at Oxford. Robert selected a site at Faringdon – a 'very pleasant situation and with good supplies' – and during the summer he built a strong castle there, manning it with the 'flower of his army'. The result was that the garrisons of the royal castles found themselves in an awkward situation – so much so that they had no alternative but to appeal to Stephen for help.

He came at once, putting aside all other commitments and bringing with him an army of several thousand men. He sat down before the castle of Faringdon in the summer of 1145, determined to take it at all costs. He did indeed go to unusual lengths in bringing up siege engines of 'wonderful power', stationing his archers in a ring all round the castle, constantly hurling javelins at the defenders and making daring assaults on the ramparts, regardless of danger.

Robert's men put up a firm resistance, but in the end they had no choice but to capitulate. Terms were agreed and the castle was handed over to Stephen. This victory at Faringdon was said to be the 'height of his glory', and his luck did indeed seem to have changed from this time onwards. Things began to go consistently well for him, while Matilda's supporters, disheartened by this latest setback, showed themselves less and less willing to enter battle for her. A number of them, to protect their own interests, made their peace with Stephen, among them the ever-adaptable Ranulf of Chester. He had been staging minor rebellions against Stephen in the north, but now he nimbly changed sides once again. Another defection must have been the cause of considerable pain to Robert of Gloucester, for his own son Philip went over to Stephen and was soon fighting against his father with the same savagery as he had shown when fighting on his side.

Ranulf of Chester seemed anxious to demonstrate his new devotion to the King, first of all helping him to capture Bedford, and then going on with him to harass the castle of Wallingford, which was still holding out under Brian fitzCount. They even swore great oaths of friendship one to the other; but Stephen could hardly be blamed if he felt little more confidence in Ranulf than he had felt in Geoffrey de Mandeville. He preserved an outward show of good fellowship, but in reality he was watching him carefully, and waiting to see how things turned out.

Matilda, meanwhile, had become so alarmed by these developments that she was driven to make overtures of peace; but since even then she was not prepared to make any serious concessions, and since Stephen, with everything going well for him, had not the slightest intention of giving way on any point, nothing came of the negotiations. The year 1145 ended with no conclusion to the struggle in sight, but with the balance tipped against Matilda.

11 Henry fitzEmpress

Stephen became more and more distrustful of Ranulf of Chester, for although he seemed friendliness itself, he had still not surrendered any of the castles he had previously seized by force, nor had he given any pledges of his good faith. The crisis was precipitated in 1146 by Ranulf himself, who arrived at Stephen's court with a sorry tale to tell. He was being harassed by enemies, he said, in particular by bands of savage Welshmen who were invading his lands, laying waste his crops and burning the towns. He and his men would be driven to extremities, he maintained, if the King did not come to his aid. It would cost him nothing, for Ranulf himself would pay all expenses, and it would not even take the King long. 'The mere sound of the King's name', he proclaimed grandiloquently, 'will strike these miscreants with terror. His mere presence will inspire greater fear than many thousands of soldiers.'

Stephen, perhaps flattered, seemed to be rather attracted by the idea, but his advisers told him it would be madness to go off into the wilds of Wales when he had plenty to do dealing with insurrections at home. It would be very dangerous, as well, to lead an army through narrow passes and forests where he could so easily be ambushed. He would be wise to remember Ranulf's record. He was friendly enough now, but he should be forced to give hostages to guarantee his continued loyalty. In fact, he should be asked to do so straight away, and if he refused so reasonable a request, then he was obviously an enemy at heart and should be arrested.

Stephen could not make up his mind what to do, so his barons took the initiative and told Ranulf that the King would not help him against the Welsh unless he handed over hostages without delay. Ranulf, taken by surprise, said it was not for this that he had come to court, that he had been given no notice of these demands and had therefore had no opportunity of consulting his friends.

The course of events now developed a deadly familiarity. There was a contrived quarrel, as there had been at Oxford, and again at St Alban's, and Ranulf, who was in the King's 'peace', was seized, put in chains and flung into prison.

Some of Ranulf's supporters were so infuriated by this that they flew to arms, but the more sober and sensible of them came to Stephen to negotiate terms for his release. They offered to hand over the castles which Stephen claimed to be his by right, including the castle of Lincoln, to which Stephen attached symbolic importance as the scene of his defeat, and also to give hostages in return for Ranulf's release. Stephen agreed to these terms provided that Ranulf swore a solemn oath that he would never again take up arms against him.

He did so, and was set at liberty. At once, outraged by Stephen's treachery, as he saw it, he launched once more into rebellion. Whether it was genuinely outraged innocence, or angry frustration at the failure of a plot, is not certain. Henry of Huntingdon thought him innocent, and certainly Ranulf had no particular reason to change over to Matilda's side at this time, as she did not seem to be winning. On the other hand, weak as Matilda's position was in England, her situation in Normandy had been transformed over the last few years; and Ranulf possessed lands in Normandy.

Geoffrey had been making steady progress since Robert of Gloucester's hurried departure to England in 1142 to rescue his sister besieged in Oxford. Avranches had submitted to him, and he had received homage from the lords of the neighbouring castles. He had then advanced on the Cotentin and by the end of the year 1143 he had taken Verneuil and was in control of all the country south and west of the Seine. The great capital city of

Rouen was his next objective, and in January 1144 he crossed
the Seine at Vernon with a large army. He marched north-west
and pitched his camp at La Trinité du Mont, close to the walls
of Rouen, on the following day. The citizens opened their gates
to him and escorted him in solemn procession to the cathedral,
in spite of a gale so violent that it flattened the woodlands for
miles around and blew down a number of houses. The keeper of
the castle, however, was a supporter of Stephen and he refused
to submit to Geoffrey.

The castle of Rouen was a formidable stronghold and although
a number of the barons, including his new ally Waleran of
Meulan, came to his aid, Geoffrey did not succeed in taking it for
a further three months, by which time hunger had reduced the
garrison to the last extremes of despair. The surrender of Rouen
castle gave Geoffrey control of Normandy, and he was able to
deal quickly with the few remaining centres of resistance. He
made no bones, however, about this triumph being entirely his
own. He was now Duke of Normandy, for he had won the title
by force of arms, and he clearly had no thought of handing over
the Duchy to his wife, the legal heiress.

None the less, he had gained almost as much for her as for
himself by his victories, for nearly all the great barons of England
held lands in Normandy, and with Geoffrey firmly in control,
they obviously risked losing them if they supported Stephen too
enthusiastically. Self-interest kept many of them loyal to Matilda
when otherwise they might have deserted to what looked like
the winning side in England.

Stephen seemed pleased at first by the way he had dealt with
Ranulf of Chester, and he kept his Christmas court of 1146 in a
spirit of triumph at Lincoln. He did it in defiance of a local
superstition that it was unlucky for a king to wear his crown in
that city. He saw to it that his court was particularly brilliant and
splendid; but his nobles did not forget that he had once again
demonstrated that he was not to be trusted, and that men who
attended his court were not safe from attack. Potential defectors
became the more wary of putting themselves in his power, and

Stephen began to lose the support of men who might otherwise
have joined him.

Ranulf continued to attack the King, with varying fortunes,
and at the least he succeeded in making a considerable nuisance
of himself. He succeeded in something else as well. Sympathy
with Ranulf and indignation at Stephen's treatment of the Empress Matilda's supporters seem to have been responsible for
inducing her son to set out on an expedition to England. Henry
had returned to Angers, probably early in 1144, and now, in 1147,
when he was not yet fourteen years old, he felt the time had come
to lead an invasion of his own. It seems incredible that his father
should have allowed him, totally inexperienced as he was, to put
himself at the head of an army and embark on such a difficult and
dangerous venture. Perhaps Geoffrey thought experience cheap
at any price, but at least he does not seem to have encouraged
him by giving him money to mount the expedition.

Henry fitzEmpress crossed the Channel and landed, probably at
Wareham. The rumour instantly spread that he had brought
many thousands of men with him, that he had huge sums of
money at his disposal, and that he had over-run one district and
committed another to the flames. Matilda's supporters were
delighted. A 'new light' seemed to have burst upon their astonished
vision, while the King's men were correspondingly depressed.
Gradually, however, the fact began to emerge that Henry had
come not with an army but with a small body of troops, and that
they were receiving no pay at all but were relying on promises of
spoils to come. It was also said that Henry and his men had
scored no positive successes but were just idling about. This
last sounds unlikely behaviour for Henry, who was nothing if
not energetic, but he may have been inhibited by lack of funds
and uncertainty about what to do next.

He eventually made an attack on Cricklade and 'Burtuna'
(probably Bourton) but failed to take either of them. By this time,
his men seem to have become impatient for the promised spoils,
and some of them went off and left him, while the others began to
demand money, and at once.

He appealed to his mother for help, but she excused herself, saying, perhaps truly enough, that all her treasure was gone. It is one of the puzzling features of this thoroughly puzzling affair that Matilda seems to have made no effort at all to stop such a foolhardy enterprise when she heard of it. At the least she might have been expected to send some commander of experience to help and advise her son. Henry then turned to his uncle Robert of Gloucester, but he, 'squatting greedily over his money-bags', as a contemporary chronicler unkindly puts it, preferred to keep his money for himself. This imputation of miserliness seems grossly unfair since Robert must have poured out a fortune in supporting his sister's cause over the years. It is more likely that he thought the whole expedition a nonsense which should not be encouraged.

In the event, Henry demonstrated that however short of money he might be, he certainly did not lack nerve, for he sent to King Stephen, of all people, and begged him from the goodness of his heart, and in consideration of their close ties of kinship, to get him out of his difficulties. Stephen, reverting to his rôle of chivalrous knight, sent Henry, almost incredibly, the money he asked for. Henry, accordingly, was able to pay off his troops and go home to Normandy, arriving about the end of May 1147.

It is an extraordinary story. How could it come about that Stephen was willing to pay the military expenses of a young man who had come over to England specifically to fight against him and take away his crown? He may have calculated, perhaps, that the money was well spent if it would get the boy out of the country, for there was always the chance that he might become a focus of revolt; or the sheer effrontery of Henry's appeal may have amused him so much that he could not resist granting it.

It is tantalising that there is no record of what Matilda felt about Henry's first effort in making war. She must have been proud, one imagines, at his sheer courage and enterprise, however unrealistic the whole affair must have seemed. And Geoffrey, that rather enigmatic figure – what of him? Again, silence. Nothing is known of how he greeted his son on his return or of what he thought of the whole adventure.

On 31 October of that same year 1147, Robert of Gloucester died very suddenly. Matilda must have felt the loss deeply, both on personal grounds and as a crippling blow to her cause. He had been loyal to her without reserve, she had depended on him, and without his help she could not go on. She left England early in the following year, 1148, and went to live quietly with her husband and children in Rouen. This did not mean, however, that she had given up hope that the crown of England could still be won, if not for herself, then for her son, and she followed the news from England as it filtered through to her across the Channel with passionate concern; and she was, naturally, pleased to learn that Stephen had got himself into fresh difficulties with the Church.

, The trouble was in part due to, or at any rate exacerbated by, the startling rise to fame and influence of the future Saint Bernard of Clairvaux. He was famous for his austerity, for his uncomfortably high standards of Christian rectitude and for his readiness to rebuke kings and princes, and even Popes, if they failed to do what he considered to be their duty. He was a Cistercian monk, the reforming order which had made a cult of poverty, self-mortification and harsh asceticism, and from his bare, uncomfortable cell in the monastery at Citeaux issued one of the most powerful voices in Christendom. He was startlingly successful in getting people to obey him. He preached the Second Crusade, calling on Christian warriors to stop fighting among themselves and to take up arms to free Jerusalem from the infidel. Almost at once, amid scenes of hysterical enthusiasm, all manner of men vowed themselves to this sacred mission, including the Emperor Conrad and King Louis of France, as well as any number of unlikely Christian warriors such as Waleran of Meulan, William of Warenne, and the turncoat son of Robert of Gloucester.

Bernard of Clairvaux did not only concern himself with great movements, he also kept an inquisitive and vigilant eye on the minutiae of Church affairs all over Europe. In particular, he had a passionate dislike of Henry, Bishop of Winchester; that 'old whore of Winchester', as he called him. Like another future saint, Thomas Becket, there was nothing 'meek and mild' about Bernard, and he was a great hater. There was one matter in particular in English church affairs about which he felt strongly, and that was the choice of a successor to Thurstan, Archbishop of York, who had died in 1140. The question of the succession turned into a long and complicated dispute which was not finally settled for a number of years.

First of all, Stephen and Bishop Henry between them managed to secure the election of their nephew Henry de Sully, the son of their inadequate older brother William. He had already been made Abbot of Fécamp, and modelling himself on his uncle Henry, who had kept Glastonbury when he became Bishop of Winchester, he refused to give it up. But he was not a man of his uncle's calibre and times had changed. So he lost his chance. The Pope ordered a new election and this time Henry of Winchester backed another of his relatives, William fitzHerbert, the son of his half-sister. There was nothing against William personally and at the insistence of the King he was formally elected by a majority of the chapter of York. A minority, however, absolutely refused to accept him, and they were backed by the Cistercians, who were in turn supported by Bernard of Clairvaux. He gave his support to the rival nominee, Henry Murdac, a fellow Cistercian who had been a monk at Clairvaux.

A long series of diplomatic manœuvres then followed, and the feud between Bernard and Henry of Winchester grew ever more virulent. 'Behold, here, here I say is the enemy!' wrote Bernard in one of his many letters to the Pope. 'Here is the man who walks before Satan, the son of perdition, the man who disrupts all rights and laws. This is the man who has "set his face against the heavens", who has repudiated, reprobated, rejected and renounced the just judgement of the apostle, confirmed, consolidated, promulgated and clearly defined in solemn conclave.' His style was distinctly wordy.

Henry of Winchester had been in a strong position at the start

as he had been Papal Legate and had consecrated his nominee in
defiance of Bernard; but in 1143 Pope Innocent II died and
Henry's legatine authority came to an end. Two new Popes
followed each other in quick succession and there seemed to be
stalemate at York; but in 1145 Pope Eugenius III, who had been
one of Bernard's own monks, was elected, and he naturally
tended to favour Bernard's nominee. Early in 1147, the unfortun-
ate William, whose only crime lay in the fact that he was a
protégé of Henry of Winchester, was displaced and a new
election ordered. The result was a dead heat between Hilary, a
new candidate, and Henry Murdac, still waiting in the wings.
Pope Eugenius came down in favour of Henry Murdac, Bernard's
protégé, and in December of that same year, he was consecrated
and given his pallium. Hilary was elected Bishop of Chichester
by way of consolation.

Stephen had acted quite correctly at the beginning of the
dispute, but the powerful Bernard's virulent and sustained attack
on Stephen's brother inevitably rubbed off on Stephen to some
extent. Worse still, Bernard now began to view Stephen himself
with suspicion, if not hostility. Stephen, for his part, felt that he
had been treated at the very least with discourtesy and that his
royal prerogative had been infringed. Thoroughly provoked by
this time, he refused to recognise Henry Murdac and diverted
the income from his see to the royal treasury. He had the backing
of the citizens of York, who disliked Henry Murdac, refused to
let him enter the city and set on anyone who came to visit him.
In the end, Murdac retired to Ripon and retaliated by laying
York under interdict, a sentence which was firmly ignored by
all the citizens.

Early in 1148, Eugenius III decided to hold a Church Council
at Rheims and summoned the English bishops to attend –
in particular, of course, Theobald, Archbishop of Canterbury.
Stephen, still feeling irritated with the Pope, forbade his bishops
to go, citing the 'ancient customs of the realm' by which it was
necessary for them to get the King's permission before leaving
the country. He then relented a little and gave three bishops

leave to attend; they were Robert of Hereford, William of Norwich and Hilary of Chichester.

Stephen suspected that Theobald of Canterbury might attempt to disobey him, so he had the Archbishop watched and all the ports carefully guarded. Theobald, however, managed to outwit him. He had already hired a small fishing smack which he had hidden in an isolated creek, and when the time came, he eluded the King's guards. Accompanied by his clerk, Thomas Becket, he made his way to the coast and somehow survived the crossing in his not very sea-worthy boat. He arrived, in fact, as one 'swimming rather than sailing', said the Pope.

The Pope was naturally very pleased with him and showed him particular favour; a favour which Theobald clearly deserved. A general sentence of excommunication had been launched against all those who had failed to attend the Council, but Theobald pleaded, unsuccessfully, for Henry of Winchester to be spared. This showed great magnanimity, for Henry had been pulling every possible string during the last few years to get archiepiscopal status for Winchester, and if he had succeeded, this would have had the effect of diminishing Theobald's own authority in the English Church.

Then it was the King's turn. Pope Eugenius had decided to excommunicate Stephen, and the candles were already lit, ready to be dashed to the ground as sentence was pronounced, when Theobald suddenly intervened and pleaded for mercy. Eugenius was much moved.

'Regard him carefully, brethren,' he said, 'for he shows the true character of the Man of the Gospels. He loves his enemies and prays for those who persecute him.'

It was agreed that the sentence should be suspended for three months, during which time the King must give satisfaction for his misdeeds, but Stephen was far from intending any such thing. As soon as Theobald was back in Canterbury, he sent a message to him demanding an explanation of his disobedience, and when no satisfactory explanation was forthcoming, he ordered him to leave the country. Theobald had no choice but to obey, and he sailed from Dover in the company of his friend Gilbert Foliot, Abbot of Gloucester. They took up residence in the Abbey of St Bertin at St Omer, and while they were there Theobald caused further outrage to Stephen by consecrating Gilbert Bishop of Hereford. This was done with the approval of Matilda's son Henry, who gave his consent on condition that fealty should be sworn to him, and not to Stephen. It was no wonder that Stephen was angry, for the fact that the approval of Henry fitzEmpress had been asked almost suggested that Theobald was regarding him as heir to the throne. Moreover, England was now laid under interdict; but here Stephen triumphed, for the sentence was almost entirely disregarded except in the diocese of Canterbury.

After all this, Theobald was hardly welcome when he returned to England, but eventually a reconciliation was patched up and, although Stephen had given no satisfaction and made no apology, the interdict was lifted. All the same, he had given serious offence to the Church, and he paid a price for it later.

Knowing as he did, only too well, the difficulties of a disputed succession, Stephen was very anxious that his son Eustace should be crowned in his own lifetime, and the only person who could do it was the Archbishop of Canterbury. But would he? Stephen was still stubbornly refusing to accept Murdac as Archbishop of York – another point against him – while Theobald was equally stubborn in quoting the dictum of Pope Celestine II that no 'innovation' should be made regarding the succession to the English throne.

Theobald's refusal was, of course, vitally important to Matilda for it affected the prospects of her own son, who decided in 1149 that he would make another expedition to England. Ostensibly he went to be knighted by King David of Scotland, but his real intention was to stir up trouble for Stephen when and where he could. King David had made a point of putting an end to his long quarrel with Ranulf of Chester who, always ready for rebellion and adventure, declared himself willing to adopt Henry's cause. Unfortunately, however, the supporters of the Angevin party were by this time fragmented and few of them were in the mood to embark on a fresh bout of civil war. Henry and King David, together with their new ally Ranulf, advanced to the outskirts of York, but Stephen was there before them and both sides seemed to prefer to avoid a pitched battle.

Henry then made for Hereford, travelling by little-known byways, for he realised that he ran a considerable risk of capture. Indeed he came very near it on the next stage of his journey, for Eustace, the King's son, learning that Henry was spending the night at Dursley castle, near Stroud, on his way south to Bristol, laid ambushes for him in three separate places. Henry, however, was warned in time and fled from the castle in the middle of the night. He reached Bristol safely but achieved nothing very much afterwards, apart from capturing Bridport, and he returned to Normandy in January 1150. Geoffrey, however, considered that Henry had now proved himself a soldier and a leader of men, and recognised this fact by declaring him of age, when he returned, and handing over to him the Duchy of Normandy. Matilda had already withdrawn her own claim to the Duchy in her son's favour.

Henry did not return to a life of peace for he was soon embroiled in quarrels with the King of France. After various indecisive encounters, Louis gathered an army at full strength and in August 1151 advanced down the Seine. Geoffrey and Henry drew up their forces on the borders of Normandy in readiness to resist him, and it looked as though an outright war was inevitable.

It never happened. Louis was taken ill, and the delay in hostilities gave a chance for conciliators on both sides to get to work, Bernard of Clairvaux apparently at the head of them, and terms of peace were arranged. Henry gave up his claim to the Norman Vexin, and in return Louis recognised him as Duke of Normandy. After that, Henry, accompanied by Geoffrey and Matilda, went to Paris, and there he did homage to Louis as his overlord in Normandy.

There also he met Eleanor of Aquitaine, Louis's beautiful but unmanageable wife. She had been a great heiress at the time of her marriage, for she had inherited all the land from the Loire to

the foothills of the Pyrenees, and from the central uplands of the
Auvergne to the western coast. She had grown up in a brilliant
and sophisticated society, and in Aquitaine she had been a patron
of poets and scholars. She was fifteen when she married Louis,
and no bridegroom could have been less suitable to her in
temperament. Louis was rather immature and exceedingly pious;
so much so that he would press himself against the wall to allow
a priest to pass in front of him. 'I have married a monk, not a
monarch!' exclaimed Eleanor furiously.

Louis's damp and gloomy castle on the Seine seemed to her a
poor exchange for her father's sunny lands in the south, and
instead of the witty conversation she was used to, she had to
listen to long, boring monologues from bishops.

When Louis went on Crusade in 1147, Eleanor absolutely
refused to be left behind. She recruited a regiment of similarly
warlike women and rode at their head on a white charger,
flourishing lance and battle-axe. She was clearly going to be a
considerable nuisance to the Crusaders, but Louis, who was still
besottedly in love with her, could refuse her nothing; and in any
case she was quite out of his control.

She turned out to be even more of a handicap than she had
promised to be, choosing camp sites for their amenities rather
than their military suitability, and when she and Louis reached
Antioch, she caused scandal by apparently falling in love with
her fascinating uncle, Raymond, Prince of Antioch. He was
handsome, gay and amusing, and only eight years older than she
was. There is no certain proof that they were lovers, but it is
certain that they spent many hours together chatting in the
Poitevin dialect which nobody else could understand. Soon
Eleanor was more discontented than ever with her dull husband.

She then hit on a brilliant idea, perhaps inspired by Raymond.
She informed Louis that she had but lately realised that they were
related in a degree forbidden by the Church. Their marriage,
therefore, was sinful, their souls in jeopardy. Was this perhaps
the reason that they had so far had no son? The whole matter,
she told him, was preying on her mind unbearably.

She had chosen the exactly right argument to use, for Louis, pious before all else and an obedient son of the Church, was now in torment. Must he choose between his religion and his wife; his wife whom he dearly loved? He turned to his advisers, who told him briskly that the whole thing was nonsense, and that there must be no question of losing Eleanor and her immensely valuable inheritance. In action, they were brisker still, for they seized her one night, and by morning she found herself removed from Antioch and her dangerously charming uncle.

The Pope, too, took a firm line when they visited him on their way home. Louis consulted him about this worrying problem of consanguinity, and he told them categorically not to give it another thought. He personally confirmed their marriage, ordered a luxurious couch to be prepared for them, and saw them into bed together.

By the time Geoffrey and his son arrived in Paris in 1151, Eleanor was nearing thirty, still beautiful, still discontented. Geoffrey was now thirty-eight – Geoffrey 'the Handsome'. His son Henry was eighteen, never particularly handsome, but undeniably attractive. They made a dangerous trio, and Eleanor seems to have found herself greatly attracted by both of them; a situation watched sourly, no doubt, by Matilda, who was by this time nearing fifty, and a disappointed, frustrated woman. It must have been watched equally sourly by Louis; if, that is, he noticed, in his unworldly way, what was going on under his nose.

It was conspicuous enough, for Eleanor, evidently deciding that the father was the more attractive of the two, seems to have made no secret of her feelings for him. He, too, paid marked attention to her; she would have been difficult to resist. Almost certainly they became lovers – it seems likely on the past record of both of them, but there is no firm evidence. There *is* evidence, however, that Matilda left the French court on her own, perhaps because of the humiliating position in which she found herself.

She was never to see Geoffrey again. He left Paris in early September and on the way home, the weather being hot, he plunged into a river to cool himself. This was blamed for the fact that he developed a high fever and died on 7 September 1151 at Château-du-Loir.

It cannot be supposed that Matilda grieved for him. He had had some good qualities and she was certainly in his debt for winning back the Duchy of Normandy for her, but however good-looking and charming, he had a cold nature. In any case, they were incompatible and had never been happy together.

If she did not grieve overmuch for Geoffrey, however, she may well have been upset by his will and the highly unpleasant scenes it occasioned, for while Geoffrey had made Henry his heir to Anjou, the laid down that if ever Henry should succeed to the English throne, then he was to give up Anjou and hand it over to his younger brother Geoffrey. Fearing, however, and with some reason, that Henry would never part with Anjou once he had got possession of it, Geoffrey ordered that his body was not to be buried until Henry had made a solemn vow that he would obey his father's wishes.

Henry was outraged. He found it unendurable. He could by no means consent to anything so monstrous as to give away half his rightful inheritance.

So his father's body lay unburied.

Henry stormed and he wept. No doubt he created unparalleled scenes of fury and indignation; he was always to be able to do that. He appealed to everybody in sight to witness the injustice of what was asked of him.

And still the body lay unburied, no doubt beginning to smell by this time.

He was told that it would be a deep and lasting disgrace to him if his father's body were allowed to fall into corruption and denied the rites of burial. So in the end, there was nothing for it. Henry made his solemn vow, still weeping and protesting, and his father was buried at last, with all pomp and ceremony, in the cathedral of Le Mans; but Henry did not keep his promise.

12 My Son and Heir in All Things

Queen Eleanor of France had by no means forgotten her plans for a divorce, and neither had Louis, whose conscience continued to plague him in spite of the reassurances of the Pope. The first practical steps towards a divorce were taken at Christmas 1151 when Louis withdrew his garrisons from Eleanor's territory in Aquitaine. In March of the following year a Church Council was held, with Archbishop Hugh of Sens presiding, at which the marriage of Louis and Eleanor was dissolved on the grounds of consanguinity. Eleanor was free.

She was also at risk. She was still quite young, she was extremely beautiful, and, more desirable still from a marriage point of view, she was the owner of vast lands and a huge fortune. Her journey south to her own territory was adventurous. The young Count Theobald of Blois, the son of Stephen's older brother, made an attempt to kidnap her during the first night of her journey and she had to flee to the city of Tours. Henry's younger brother Geoffrey was not to be left out, and he laid an ambush for her on the frontiers of Touraine. Fortunately, she got word of it in advance and travelled by another route, so arriving safely in her own lands.

She had already decided on the husband she wanted; she wanted Henry, and she wrote to him to offer him her hand. He accepted – he would have been mad to do anything else – and they were married very quietly at Poitiers on 18 May 1152.

It is easy to take the obvious and cynical line of saying that the marriage was a purely political affair. Henry acquired Aquitaine and Gascony, an enormous increase for him in power and wealth. From Eleanor's point of view, Henry, already Duke of Normandy and Count of Anjou, and perhaps to be King of England, was easily the most eligible husband available at the time. But there may very well have been more to it than that. Eleanor was not only beautiful, she was witty, intelligent and charming as well. Henry may have been extremely jealous when, at the French court the year before, Eleanor had preferred his father; but the fact that she was almost certainly Geoffrey's mistress does not mean that she had been unaware of Henry. He was an impressive figure by any standards, vigorous, spirited and thoroughly masculine. There was over ten years difference in age between them, but that was of no importance at this time. Henry, even at eighteen, was mature and experienced, and Eleanor was probably at the peak of her beauty. Years later, when she was nearing middle age, a poet who merely caught a passing glimpse of her wrote:

> *Were the world to be mine*
> *From the sea to the Rhine*
> *With it all I would part*
> *If next to my heart*
> *Lay England's queen . . .*

Other versifiers were not so kind, for the marriage, coming only a matter of weeks after the divorce, caused considerable scandal. Robert of Gloucester (the chronicler, not the earl) believed that Henry and Eleanor had been lovers while she was still married to Louis:

> *He was much acquaint with the Queen of France*
> *Some deal too much, as me weaned; so that in some thing*
> *The Queen loved him, as me trowed, more than her lord the King.*

Walter Map maintained that Eleanor had cast lascivious eyes on Henry when he had been in Paris and that she had engineered the divorce in order to marry him, but it is, of course, a fact that Eleanor had been wanting a divorce some time before she had ever met Henry.

Nothing is recorded of what Matilda thought of her new daughter-in-law, but her natural reaction would have been one of outrage. Eleanor was by now notorious. The King of France, a simple-minded man whose eyes had been opened at last to what his wife was like, had declared that even the meanest of his subjects would not care to marry her. Matilda might not have worried overmuch about Eleanor's reputation in general, but she could not have failed to be angry when she remembered that her own husband Geoffrey had probably been the latest of her lovers. Now this woman was the wife of her beloved son Henry. She must also have recalled that there had been some discussion, when they had been at the French court, of a possible marriage between Henry and one of Eleanor's two daughters. It was all a little reminiscent of the later Roman Emperors and their complicated family relationships.

On the other hand Matilda was enough of a realist to appreciate the immense political advantages of the marriage. Whatever her feelings may have been, she seems to have controlled them well enough on the surface, for when Henry went to England in 1153, he left Eleanor, who was by this time pregnant, in Matilda's care, a thing he would surely not have done if they had not been on reasonably good terms.

Eleanor's standards of behaviour as a wife, however, had apparently not improved very much since her days with Louis, for quite soon there was gossip about her relationship with the poet Bernard de Ventadour, who declared that he trembled like an aspen leaf in her presence, and wrote her poems of love and longing:

> *When the sweet breeze*
> *Blows hither from your dwelling*
> *Methinks I feel*
> *A breath of Paradise.*

Henry, however, was a very different kind of husband from Louis. He abruptly sent for Bernard to come to England and told him that for the future he was to confine his poetic Muse to tales of martial exploits only.

Louis, however disillusioned with Eleanor, was far from pleased by her marriage to Henry. He was, in fact, extremely angry. He had been resigned to losing Aquitaine when he lost Eleanor, but it had apparently never occurred to him that the already powerful Duke of Normandy might acquire her lands in his place. There was the further consideration that if Eleanor should bear a son, the two daughters she had had by Louis would be disinherited.

Louis had a reasonable complaint against Henry in that by feudal law an heiress could not marry without the consent of her overlord, so he sent for Henry to appear before his court and explain his conduct. Henry, however, now felt strong enough to defy the French King and he refused to acknowledge the authority of his court or appear before it.

Meanwhile, Stephen's son Eustace had seized this favourable moment to visit the King of France, and his long-projected marriage to Constance, the King's sister, at last took place. Henry, who was on the point of sailing for England from Barfleur, suddenly found himself faced with a hastily patched-up alliance between Louis, Eustace and several other magnates, among them his own brother Geoffrey. Their aim was to seize all his possessions on the Continent and divide them up between themselves. Abandoning his plans to leave for England, Henry marched against them. Some indecisive fighting took place with nothing much achieved on either side until Henry captured and burnt several castles, before going on to lay siege to the castle of Montsoreau on the Loire, where most of the allies, including Geoffrey, had established themselves. Henry was successful in taking the castle, and Geoffrey was forced to agree to Henry's terms. Louis then lost interest in the struggle, and a truce was agreed, leaving Henry once more free to sail for England.

By this time it had become urgent for him to cross the Channel, and even when Louis promptly broke the truce, he did not allow it to stop him. There had been little military activity in England since Henry had left it in 1150 as the barons had become thoroughly sick of fighting, and although they sometimes attacked a castle here or there, nothing of importance was achieved. As for Stephen, he had been devoting more of his energies to persuading Archbishop Theobald to crown Eustace than to anything else. But still Theobald refused; still he quoted Pope Celestine's letter forbidding any 'innovation'. It may be that he was also influenced by his estimate of Eustace's character. He seems to have been a violent, unprincipled sort of man with nothing much to recommend him but his prowess in war. In a last bid to win Theobald over, Stephen had even sacrificed his own candidate to the see of York, and had recognised Henry Murdac; but it made no difference. Theobald still steadfastly refused to crown Eustace.

In 1152, Stephen, desperate by this time, took all the English bishops prisoner and locked them up. They were afraid for their lives, remembering that Stephen had 'never much cared for bishops'; but they remained firm in their refusal to crown his son in spite of threats and hardship. And in the end, of course, he had to let them go.

Frustrated by this encounter with the Church, Stephen turned once more to the task of subduing the rebels who were still active against him. The strongest fortress of all, the castle of Wallingford, which had been a trouble to him ever since Brian fitzCount had declared for Matilda, was still holding out; but Brian fitzCount himself was dead.

He died, nobody knows how, or why, or where, some time between 1147 and September 1151. Like so many prominent people of the time, a great deal is known of him in some ways, and nothing at all in others. In the brief glimpses we have of him, he appears as a particularly vivid and engaging character, but the gaps are much larger than the fragments of knowledge. Even his birth and ancestry are not entirely certain. He was probably, but not certainly, the natural son of Alan Fergant of Brittany. But who was his mother? He was treated with great kindness by Henry I; a debt he repaid in loyalty to the King's daughter. But did he love her for her own sake as well, as one

chronicler hinted? There is no certain answer. Henry gave Brian
an heiress for his wife, but what sort of woman was she? They
are said to have had no children, but according to one account,
Brian had two sons who were lepers; a sad little footnote. And
that is all that is known of his personal life.

One thing is certain, however, and that is that he did all in his
power to support Matilda not only by the sword, but in other
ways as well. Apart from his correspondence with the Bishop of
Winchester, he is known to have written some sort of 'book' or
pamphlet in support of the Angevin cause, for a letter from
Gilbert Foliot to Brian has survived in which he speaks of it.

'Some people,' writes Gilbert, 'have been very much surprised
because although you are not a man of letters, you have none the
less brought out a book. It is no miracle to me, for I know that
the passionate enthusiasm you feel for your subject makes up for
anything you may lack in formal studies. And I may say that you
have made no mean entry into the literary field.'

After deploring the broken vows of all those who had sworn
to recognise Matilda, Gilbert remarks that Brian had been the
exception; what he had promised in words, he had guarded most
faithfully in his heart. It was true; in an age of self-seeking,
treachery and sheer villainy, here was a man who sought nothing
for himself, but sacrificed everything for the cause in which he
believed.

Now he was gone, and Stephen resolved that at last he would
take his castle. In 1152, he brought a large force to Wallingford,
he built fortifications at Crowmarsh, on the other side of the river
from the castle, and he succeeded in blocking all approaches to the
bridge over which supplies for the castle had to pass. The
defenders held out bravely for some time, but at last they were
reduced to such straits that they sent messages to Henry fitz-
Empress asking him to come to their aid, or else to give them
permission to surrender with honour. The whole Angevin cause
in England, they told him, was at risk if he did not come quickly.
It was this message which decided Henry to leave Normandy
without further delay in spite of the continued threat from Louis.

With a brisk breeze behind him, Henry landed in England in early January 1153 and at once 'the earth quivered with sudden rumours like reeds shaken in the wind'. Those who supported the Angevin cause were disappointed that Henry had come with only a comparatively small force; in fact, he had brought with him one hundred and forty knights and three thousand foot soldiers. Stephen's supporters were relieved that it was no larger. Both sides were impressed by his courage in braving the dangers of a stormy crossing in midwinter.

He was greeted with a favourable omen right at the start, for while attending mass after he landed, he heard the words, 'Behold the Lord, the ruler, is come and the kingdom is in his hand.' He made first of all for Malmesbury, Stephen's most important stronghold in the West Country, and his army grew as he marched. He took the town by storm, but the castle held out and he was forced to settle down to a siege. He had already achieved a success, however, in that he had drawn Stephen away from his operations in the east, and had brought him hurrying to the relief of Malmesbury with a large force. Stephen arrived by way of Cirencester and camped to the north of the river Avon with the firm intention of giving battle next day.

As so often before, however, the barons of his army were remarkably unenthusiastic. They had not refused the call to fight for their feudal lord, but they did not care very much who won the battle, and many of them were inclined to regard Henry as the rightful heir to the throne in any case. They made a 'splendid and formidable appearance', according to Henry of Huntingdon, 'their banners glittering with gold', but they were far from warlike in their intentions. Led probably by Robert of Leicester, who was soon to follow the example of his twin brother Waleran of Meulan in going over to Henry's side, Stephen's barons made it perfectly clear that they had no heart for a battle.

The weather was terrible, for one thing. It rained unceasingly, the river was high above its banks, and a strong wind battered against them so severely that they could 'hardly support their armour or handle their spears, which were dripping wet'. Conditions were a little better for Henry, for at least the wind was at his back, but the river was none the less a formidable obstacle. Stephen later gave the difficulty of fording it as the chief reason for his ignominious retreat from Malmesbury. No longer able to endure the 'severity of the weather', wrote Henry of Huntingdon, he marched back the way he had come with nothing achieved and no battle fought. Before leaving, he had arranged that Malmesbury castle should be demolished before it was surrendered so that Henry should not be able to make use of it, but even this plan turned out a failure, for it was handed over to Henry intact.

Henry went on first to Bristol and then to Gloucester, capturing a number of strong points in the Midlands before at last, after several months, he turned towards the beleaguered castle of Wallingford. It was by this time either the end of July or the beginning of August. The garrison was desperately short of supplies and in bad shape altogether, for Stephen's new castle at Crowmarsh had been almost completely successful in cutting their supply route. Henry tried to take Crowmarsh castle by storm, but failed, and had to resign himself to the weary business of a long siege.

Stephen, meanwhile, raised a large army and, accompanied by Eustace, who had followed Henry back from Normandy, marched on Wallingford. Henry drew up his forces, which were far inferior in numbers to Stephen's, and prepared for battle. Once more there was a river between the rival armies; and once more no battle was fought.

The accounts vary in matters of detail, but they all make it clear that for one reason or another, Stephen's barons, although willing to march, drew the line at actually fighting. Some of the leading barons on both sides, in fact, seem to have met together privately and arranged the terms of a truce. It was to last for a fortnight, Stephen was to raise the siege of Wallingford and Henry that of Crowmarsh. Stephen, in addition, was to demolish Crowmarsh castle. All accounts agree that Stephen and Henry were both equally furious with their unreliable supporters, and both complained bitterly of bad faith. But if their armies would not fight, there was nothing they could do; so the truce was agreed. Stephen and Henry then had a 'private' meeting, conducted apparently from opposite banks of the river, at which some more permanent arrangements were discussed.

If Stephen and Henry were angry, Eustace was beside himself with rage, for he knew very well that his only chance of succeeding to the throne lay in the total defeat of Henry. When his father left Wallingford to lay siege to Ipswich castle – Hugh Bigod once more in revolt – he went roaring off on his own, laid waste some lands in Cambridgeshire and then pounced on the Abbey of Bury St Edmund's, devastating the country round and burning crops. One week later, he was dead; from grief, according to one author, but as a just retribution for his sins against St Edmund, according to Gervase of Canterbury. He sat down to table one day in August, took a bite of food, and was at once seized with a fit of madness, which persisted until death took him a few days later.

The best that Henry of Huntingdon could say of Eustace was that he was an 'experienced soldier', but ungodly. The author of the Anglo-Saxon Chronicle was far more forthright. 'He sped [prospered] little and by good right, for he was an evil man; wherever he was, he did more evil than good.'

His death, however, did a great deal of good for the country, for it smoothed the path to peace. Negotiations were already under way, conducted chiefly by Archbishop Theobald and Henry of Winchester. Theobald, apart from refusing to crown Eustace, had held aloof from the struggle and could claim to be reasonably impartial, while Henry had made efforts to promote peace in the past and so could be regarded as sincere in that respect at least. With Eustace dead, Stephen seemed to lose interest in the succession, and although he did have another son, he made no attempt to intervene in the negotiations on his behalf. In the end, terms of peace were agreed and on 6 November 1153 Stephen and Henry met at Winchester. 'So God granted a happy issue and peace shone forth. What boundless joy! What a happy

day!' exclaimed Henry of Huntingdon. A happy day, indeed, and
the terms agreed seemed reasonable enough.

First of all, Stephen was to recognise Henry's hereditary claim
to the kingdom of England, while Henry 'graciously conceded'
that the King should, if he wished, continue to reign for the rest of
his life. There was one condition, however. The King himself,
the bishops and the nobles were to confirm on oath that after
Stephen's death, Henry, provided he outlived him, should
succeed to the throne peacefully and without opposition. Various
detailed arrangements were made about the return of lands which
had been seized unlawfully and it was agreed that the very large
number of castles which had been put up since King Henry's
death – well over a thousand, it was estimated – should be
demolished. Thus, 'by God's mercy', said Henry of Huntingdon,
the 'gloomy night' which had darkened the realm of England was
brought to a close and 'peace dawned'.

A formal document setting out the terms of the settlement
was prepared, and it is still in existence.

'Stephen, King of England, to the archbishops, bishops,
abbots, earls, justiciars, sheriffs, barons, and to all his liegemen
of England, greeting.

'Know that I, King Stephen, have established Henry, Duke of
Normandy, as my successor in the kingdom of England, and have
recognised him as my heir by hereditary right; and thus I have
given and confirmed to him and his heirs the kingdom of England.

'The Duke, in return for this honour and gift and confirmation
which I have made to him, has done homage to me . . . He has
sworn that he will be my liegeman and that he will guard my life
and honour by every means in his power . . . I have also given
an oath of surety to the Duke that I will guard his life and honour
by every means in my power and that I will maintain him as my
son and heir in all things.'

The reference to Henry as his 'son' prompted the more ribald
to rake up old scandals and remark that perhaps he was his son
in all too literal a sense.

There then came a number of detailed provisions protecting

the inheritance of Stephen's son William, but it was laid down
that some of Stephen's most important castles should be handed
over to Henry immediately on Stephen's death. Finally the archbishops, bishops and abbots took an oath that if either Stephen
or Henry should break this agreement, they would visit on the
transgressor the 'justice of the Church' until such time as the
transgressor should have corrected his ways and returned to a
proper observation of the agreement.

It was peace. It was a sensible settlement of the long years of
civil strife which had brought England to such a miserable pass.
Stephen could end his days secure in the possession of the crown,
and Henry could go back to Normandy, secure in his inheritance.
Before he went, the leading men of the kingdom did homage to
Henry as their future lord, and he then accompanied Stephen
first to Canterbury, and then to Dover. They later went back to
Canterbury, and there Henry heard that the King's Flemish
mercenaries were plotting to murder him because, it was said,
both the Duke and peace were equally hateful to them.

Henry sailed for Normandy early in April 1154. There was, in
any case, little for him to do in England until the time came for
him to succeed to the throne. Matilda too, left behind in Normandy
with Eleanor and waiting for news, seems to have had little to do,
and perhaps no inclination to exert herself. Louis was still carrying on hostilities on the border, and in September 1153 he burnt
part of the town of Verneuil; but we do not hear of Matilda
raising an army, as she would have done in the old days, and
marching out to confront the enemy. After all, she was by now
over fifty, an advanced age for a woman of the Middle Ages, but
she seemed to recover her energy as she grew older and remained active, in the political sense at least, until her death
fourteen years later.

When at last she heard the news of Henry's triumph over
Stephen, it must have been a source of overwhelming joy to
her. He had been fighting the same battle as she had fought in
England for nine years, and his success justified all that she had
suffered then. At the same time, there must have been sadness in

her recollections of past days. Her most loyal and devoted supporters were gone now – all of them; for the future, her hopes must be entirely centred in her son.

Her first grandson had been born on the same day that Eustace had died, 17 August 1153, and one would have imagined that his birth would give her satisfaction; but perhaps the only thing that mattered to her was that her son Henry should come safe home with his future assured.

That year, 1153, had seen other deaths among the leading figures of Matilda's years in England, for Ranulf of Chester, a man of daring but scarcely a man of principle, died on 16 December. He was murdered by William Peverel, Earl of Nottingham, who gave him poisoned wine to drink. According to another version of the story, he recovered, as he had only drunk very little of the wine, but died later. In this year, too, King David of Scotland died.

Stephen lived less than a year after his reconciliation with Henry. He held his court in London at the end of September 1154, and in October he went with his friend Count Thierry of Flanders to Dover. While he was there, he was taken ill very suddenly and eight days later, on 25 October, he died.

A great deal was written about Stephen by his contemporaries, a lot is known of what he did and said, yet he remains curiously elusive. The picture that emerges most clearly is that of a man constantly smiling, pleasant to everybody. Yet there was a darker side: he was not to be trusted. He was a brave soldier, though not perhaps a good general; he was energetic and swift in action, but never far-sighted. He was certainly not a wise or a clever man – although Walter Map is unfair when he calls him 'not far off an idiot'; but he never had the stature to be a King.

One of England's greatest Kings was to follow him, however, and soon there was 'very good peace such as never was here before'. Men loved Duke Henry, it was said, for 'he did good justice'. In these turbulent times, it was not generosity men longed for in their rulers, not leniency nor the remission of taxes. The cry was always for justice, and it was justice that the new King cared for above all else.

13 Unhoped Serene

The news of Stephen's death reached Henry when he was dealing with some trouble which had arisen among the barons of Normandy, and the first thing he did was to hurry back to discuss the situation with his mother Matilda. This set a pattern for the future, for as long as she was alive, he always liked to ask her advice on any matter of importance. He also sent a message to his brothers Geoffrey and William and to all the bishops and magnates of his Duchy instructing them to meet him at Barfleur before he set sail for England. The winds were contrary, however, and a whole month passed before it was possible for him to make the crossing. Yet the peace held in England from 'fear and love of Duke Henry' and because nobody questioned that he was to be King.

It was well into December when he eventually landed in England, and he went straight to London, where he was rapturously welcomed by those Londoners who had shown themselves so disagreeable to his mother and had driven her out of their city. On the Sunday before Christmas, he was crowned with all ceremony in Westminster Abbey, the thing which Matilda had so greatly desired but never achieved.

It is not certain whether Matilda attended his coronation or not, but it seems likely that she did. She had, after all, voluntarily relinquished her own claim to the crown in her son's favour, and she was devoted to him personally. It would have given her intense pleasure to see her son crowned King of England, instead of some descendant of Stephen – 'that usurper', as Henry always called him.

Whether she was at the coronation or not, she was in Normandy soon afterwards, where she lived in a palace built by her father close to the minster of Notre Dame des Prés, just outside the walls of Rouen. She seems to have lived there in considerable luxury and some state, but her life was, to outward seeming, a quiet one.

She had become friendly with one of her half-sisters, Matilda, Abbess of Montvilliers, who was a cousin of the famous twins Waleran of Meulan and Robert of Leicester. Waleran had been originally a supporter of Stephen, but he had deserted him towards the end of his reign and had gone on Crusade. Matilda now came in contact with him again through the Abbess of Montvilliers.

It seems that Matilda had made a vow at the time of her perilous escape from Oxford castle that if she got away safely, she would build a monastery in thanksgiving. Waleran, too, had made an almost identical vow when he was near to shipwreck on the way back from Crusade. The Archbishop of Rouen, hearing of these vows made in such similar circumstances, suggested that the two should put their resources together and build one really imposing monastery, instead of two lesser ones. This they agreed to do.

The monastery was built at Valace, but when it was completed, a question arose as to who was to occupy it. The monks of Mortmer and the monks of St Marcell were both anxious for the honour, and they were soon quarrelling violently. The Abbess was far from neutral in the matter, for she was greatly attached to the Abbot of Mortmer; it was hinted, in fact, that she was his mistress. She went to Matilda to persuade her to intervene on behalf of the Mortmer monks, and Matilda obligingly told the contestants that if the matter were not settled forthwith in favour of the Mortmer monks, she would call in some different monks altogether. That was the end of the trouble.

Matilda was notably generous to the Church during these years, for she built at least two more monasteries and gave land and money to others. She also embarked on the building of a bridge over the Seine at Rouen. The existing bridge was a humble wooden affair, and she decided to build a bridge of stone with thirteen splendid arches, which should be a glory to the city.

She obviously enjoyed building as a sideline, but she had no lack of public business. Although she seemed to have passed finally from the centre of the stage, she was, in fact, virtually Regent of Normandy, charters were issued in her own and Henry's name, and he relied on her to maintain peace in the Duchy when he was away. He constantly asked her advice and he generally took it. He was anxious, for instance, to make some provision for his younger brother William, who had been left no inheritance at all by his father, and he had conceived the idea of conquering Ireland and giving it to him. He even went so far as to get authorisation for this plan from the Pope, since the Pope was regarded as the owner of all islands which had no other sovereign. Matilda, however, was very much against the scheme and advised him to give it up – as he did; surely very sound advice.

In 1160 she became ill and nearly died – the trouble seems to have been some complication of the illness she had suffered after Geoffrey's birth. Henry came hurrying to be with her, and with his advice she made gifts on a vast scale to 'churches, monasteries, and the poor', and particularly to her favourite monastery of Bec.

It was not the end for Matilda, however, and in the seven years of life remaining to her, she played a significant part in the dispute between Henry and Thomas Becket which shadowed the first half of her son's reign. And on this, she certainly gave Henry good advice.

When Henry came to the throne, his first task was to try to establish peace and good order in a land which had been rapidly sliding into anarchy. He had to put the financial affairs of the country in order, he had to see that the operation of the law, the 'King's justice', was fair and orderly, and above all, he had to get rid of the elements in the country which made for lawlessness, such as the Flemish mercenaries: wild, violent bands of men and the source of endless trouble, who were still roaming the country-side.

He was an energetic and efficient ruler, but he still needed efficient ministers to help him. He had Richard de Lucy 'the Loyal' who had been Stephen's Justiciar and was to be Henry's for very many years to come; but the post of Chancellor was unfilled.

The Chancellor was inferior in rank to the Justiciar, but his work brought him into closer contact with the King, for he was, in effect, the King's personal assistant. He was in charge of the Great Seal, so that all important documents fell under his eye, he attended meetings of the Exchequer, and he managed all the clerical work of the royal household. No matter of importance could be decided without the Chancellor being present. He was also the King's Chaplain, the chief officer of the royal chapel, so the Chancellor was always in holy orders, though not necessarily a priest or monk.

With so much business to transact, it was clear that Henry needed a Chancellor on whom he could rely, and Theobald of Canterbury was at once ready with a suggestion. He knew just the man, he said. It was Thomas Becket, a member of his household.

How much Theobald was thinking of Henry and the good of the country in making this suggestion, and how much of the interests of the Church, is not entirely clear. He seems to have suspected that some of the King's advisers were hostile to the interests of the Church, and he clearly hoped that Becket, as Chancellor, would be able to tip the balance the other way. If so, he was to be disappointed.

Thomas Becket came of a respectable, middle-class Norman family, but he was born in London, where his parents had recently moved. His father was a prosperous merchant, and Thomas was well and carefully educated. It is likely that he entered holy orders not from religious conviction, but because the Church offered the best road to advancement for a man not born into one of the great and noble families. Eventually, when he was about

F*

twenty-five years old, he was recommended to Archbishop Theobald by some friends of the family and became one of his clerks. He did very well at Canterbury from the beginning, and he soon developed such a flair for diplomacy that Theobald would often send him abroad on special missions.

Becket was, quite genuinely, a suitable choice as Chancellor, however mixed Theobald's motives may have been in recommending him. His subsequent behaviour must have come as a shock to Theobald, however, for Becket at once 'threw off the deacon' and became a courtier, richest of the rich, finest of the fine. He became a byword for magnificence. His banquets outshone all others; they certainly outshone those of the King, who did not go in for display and whose courtiers had to put up with distinctly inferior food. Henry, however, a generous-minded man, was amused rather than annoyed by his Chancellor's magnificence, and the two became great friends.

Matilda did not greatly care for Becket. As an aristocrat herself, she may not have been pleased that her son had made a friend of a comparatively low-born man. She probably found his flamboyance and ostentation distasteful. She may well, and with reason, have thought him vulgar. The one thing that is certain is that she did not think him a suitable choice, when the time came, as Archbishop of Canterbury, and she told Henry so in plain terms. This must have been the best piece of advice she ever gave him.

Theobald died in April 1161, but Henry did not make up his mind about a successor immediately; the see, in fact, was left unfilled for over a year. One of the problems which was worrying the King at the time was the question of the 'criminous clerks', those men in holy orders who committed crimes. They were able to claim the right to be tried in the Church courts, where the worst that could happen to them was that they would be stripped of their orders. This, however, was seldom done as the bishops did not like to admit that one of 'God's anointed' could be transformed back into an ordinary layman. Theoretically these men might face imprisonment, but the bishops were too lazy, or too mean, to maintain prisons, so that this was seldom a real danger. In practice, they almost always escaped with a fine, whatever they had done – a fine, where a layman might pay for the same crime with his life. It was a situation which the King, who really cared about justice, found intolerable.

Apart from the 'criminous clerks', there were other matters outstanding between Church and state which needed to be settled, and Henry thought it would be a great advantage to have an Archbishop with whom he knew he could work easily and well. If he hesitated a long time, it was probably because he knew how unpopular the choice of Becket would be in the eyes of the clergy. He was not even a priest, and had been living a worldly life.

When at last he did declare for Becket, however, he met with little serious opposition. The monks of Canterbury, who technically had the right to elect the Archbishop, were reluctant, but in the end they gave in. There was only one man who protested openly, and that was Gilbert Foliot, Bishop of Hereford.

Becket was ordained a priest on 2 June 1162, and was consecrated Archbishop on the following day in Canterbury Cathedral. He arrived on foot for the ceremony with tears streaming down his face. This was to become a common sight in the future, for he was a great weeper. His weeping, according to John of Salisbury, assumed near-miraculous proportions, and when he celebrated mass, his tears fell like rain.

As Archbishop, he became, suddenly and startlingly, a changed character. Gone was the gay, worldly Becket with his great banquets and rich attire. Now he scarcely touched food, he wore the sober habit of a monk and washed the feet of thirteen paupers every day. His nights were spent in prayer or in floggings. He had had himself flogged even when he was Chancellor, but now, more frequently than ever, his 'back was bared to the lash'.

'The King has wrought a miracle,' observed Gilbert Foliot sardonically.

It was a miracle that the King would have preferred not to have performed, for one of Becket's first actions was to return his seal of office as Chancellor. This decision, apparently, came as a complete surprise to Henry, and was an unpleasant shock. And soon there was trouble – serious trouble.

If Henry had looked to Becket to help him in clearing up the problem of the clerks who committed crimes, he was disillusioned indeed. Becket stood firmly, even fanatically, by the right of men in holy orders to be tried and sentenced in the Church courts and nowhere else.

Part of the trouble was that men in holy orders did not only include practising clerics; they also included even the humblest servants in an ecclesiastical institution. Practically anybody could get themselves admitted into minor orders, and very many people did, often men of low character. Quite half of them, remarked Henry in a moment of irritation, were 'adulterers, robbers, rapists, fire-raisers and murderers'. And all of them were set above the ordinary processes of the law.

So the King made a proposal. Let these clerks, he said in effect, be judged by the Church courts, as they were now, but if convicted of serious crime, let them be handed over to the lay courts for punishment.

It seemed a reasonable proposal and some of the bishops were inclined to agree with Henry; but Becket would have none of it. It would be to bring Christ again before Pontius Pilate, he declared; surely a strange description of men who had often committed the most odious of crimes.

The bishops, startled and alarmed, begged Becket to be moderate, but he simply accused them of cowardice. *He* was ready to embrace martyrdom at any time in defence of the Church; were *they*? Unhappily the bishops agreed to stand firm and support Becket against the King.

After this, the weary quarrel, which was to drag on for another year before reaching a climax at the Council of Northampton, was fairly launched. Becket devised his famous phrase 'saving the privileges of my order', which provided an escape clause from any agreement he made, the bishops one by one deserted him, and even the Pope gave him lukewarm encouragement. Suddenly,

Becket gave in. He withdrew his qualifying clause and promised to obey the 'ancient customs of the realm' in good faith; but he probably never foresaw that they were to be drawn up in writing, and that he would have to swear a solemn oath in public to observe them.

These were the famous 'Constitutions of Clarendon'. A Great Council was held at Clarendon, Henry's favourite hunting-lodge near Salisbury, in January 1164, and it was then that this document was produced. The 'customs' probably represented fairly enough the practice in the days of Henry 1, but some of them outraged contemporary church opinion. They included Henry's proposal for the treatment of the 'criminous clerks': an officer of the King was, in future, to watch the progress of trials in the church courts, and if a clerk were to be found guilty of serious crime, the Church must no longer protect him from due punishment under the law. Becket, with a sudden volte-face, absolutely refused to promise agreement and he withdrew his previous consent to the 'ancient customs'.

His bishops were divided and unhappy, but loyal. They would have liked to have seen some attempt at compromise, but they stood behind him. When armed men suddenly burst in on them, declaring they would avenge any insult inflicted on their lord, the King, it was not the bishops who ran away; it was Becket. He withdrew to another room; but in a short time, he came back.

'It is the King's will that I should perjure myself,' he said. 'I shall have to do penance for it as best I may.'

Becket then gave his solemn promise to observe the 'ancient customs of the realm', as drawn up in the 'Constitutions', 'honestly and without reserve'.

He was very soon breaking them, however. He made at least two attempts to leave the country without the King's permission, in clear contravention of the 'customs', and it became obvious that a major confrontation was unavoidable. It took place at the Council of Northampton in October that same year. Becket was called to answer for a breach of feudal law, was found guilty, quite properly, and was sentenced to forfeit his goods to the

King. Henry then let his anger get the better of his judgement, and demanded an account of all the money which had passed through Becket's hands as Chancellor. The bishops, in a panic by now, and terrified of the harm that might be done to the Church by an all-out quarrel with the King, begged Becket to be moderate. Some of them even pleaded with him to resign his office. He turned on them. 'Even if I were silent,' he said, 'future ages would tell of how you deserted me and left me alone in the battle.'

And so the final dramatic day dawned, with Becket arriving at the castle, carrying his own cross – an insult to Henry, since it suggested an expectation of martyrdom. In addition, Becket had appealed over the King's head to the Pope, another contravention of the 'customs' he had given his oath to observe. His perjury was by now flagrant and admitted, said Henry, and sentence must be pronounced.

This unwelcome task fell to Robert, Earl of Leicester; but Becket refused to hear him.

'I am your spiritual father, and I refuse to listen to you,' he cried. And standing up, still carrying his cross, he left the chamber amid shouts and jeers.

What the sentence was to be will never be known, but Henry, however provoked, was never a man of blood, and it is most unlikely that he intended any physical harm to Becket. Becket, however, was convinced that he was to be murdered, and that night, a night of streaming rain, he escaped from Northampton and made his way, by stages and in disguise, to the Kent coast and from there to the Continent. Eventually he found his way to the Papal Court, where the Pope somewhat reluctantly gave Becket his support. He then sent him off to lead the life of a 'simple monk' in the Abbey of Pontigny.

Becket, however, had no intention of being pushed into the background, and his behaviour was very different from that of previous exiled archbishops, who had lived quietly and caused no trouble. He was determined that his cause and his sufferings should have maximum publicity, and he set about writing letters

to anybody and everybody who might help him; among them the
Empress Matilda. She had a reputation for piety and she was
known to have considerable influence over her son. Becket may
have forgotten, however, that she was also devoted to Henry and
was most unlikely to take any step which could do him harm.

His first approach was by letter. He wrote to her in grossly
flattering terms; like Disraeli, he seems to have believed in
laying it on with a trowel. He told her that he thanked God for
making the nobility of her virtues outstrip even the nobility of
her birth, that though glorious in blood, she was yet more
glorious in good works. But although God values material
offerings, he told her, he values equally concern for the peace
and liberty of the Church, a thing 'very close to your heart', he
added.

He then turned to the delicate matter of her son's disgraceful
behaviour and the sufferings of the Church in England. The
King's demands, he said were 'unheard-of' and certainly not
according to custom. He rather spoilt the effect of this by adding
that if previous kings had indeed made such demands, then they
had had no business to do so. The Father is quick to show forgiveness, he went on, but her son the King was now in deadly
danger, for God was poised to strike, and soon the arrows of
death would be loosed upon her son if he did not set the Church
free – the Church which was now being 'trampled underfoot'.

Matilda was unlikely to be greatly influenced by anything which
Becket could say to her for she had never liked him or wanted
him to be Archbishop. On the other hand, she had considerable
political sense, and she knew very well that an Archbishop in
exile, claiming to have fled in actual fear for his life, and indig-
nantly reciting the story of his wrongs, was bound to do Henry
harm. She would have been glad, of course, if some reasonable
compromise could be arranged, but she would not have sympathised with Becket's sweeping claims for the power of the
Church. In her own few months of power, she had certainly
shown no disposition to surrender any of her regal rights.

So far as is known, she sent no reply to Becket's letter, but she later received an emissary from Becket who brought her another letter from him.

She had been reluctant to receive this emissary, Nicholas of Mont St Jacques, but eventually did so, and Becket's letter, when she was persuaded to read it, seemed to have a mollifying effect on her. According to Nicholas, she apologised for the way she had spoken of Becket in the past, and even for the advice she had given the King. She said that he had kept her in the dark about his intentions concerning the Church because he knew that she placed the liberty of the Church even above the royal will.

If true, these sentiments sound uncharacteristically humble and not at all like Matilda, particularly her remarks about her son. She then said, according to Nicholas, that she was writing to the King to ask him to let her know exactly what he intended about the Church, and about Becket.

'And then,' she said, 'if any effort of mine seems likely to bear fruit, I shall do all that I can in the interests of peace.'

Nicholas and his companions went on to visit Arnulf of Lisieux before calling once more on the Empress. They had intended to read aloud to her the famous 'Constitutions', but this scheme fell rather flat as they found at the last moment that they had lost their copy. They tried to repeat them by heart to her, but she was not satisfied with this and sent them away telling them to get another copy from Becket. Luckily, however, 'by God's will', they managed to find the missing copy and at a private meeting next day she asked them to read it aloud to her in Latin and then explain it in French. This suggests incidentally that although she was able to understand Latin, she was not fluent in it in conversation.

She approved some of the provisions; but then 'the woman is sprung from a race of despots,' said Nicholas, reporting to Becket. She did, however, express disapproval of a number of the clauses, and in particular, she thought it a mistake to commit the 'customs' to writing and to oblige the bishops to swear to obey them on oath. This, she said, was against precedent. All the same, she thought that some compromise might still be possible.

And here Nicholas came to the heart of the matter. 'You must know', he told Becket, 'that the lady Empress is very resourceful in defending her son, now talking of his concern for justice, now blaming the ill-nature of the bishops.' At this point she seems to have moved over to the attack. 'She said some things,' confessed Nicholas, 'with which we could not but agree.' She had shown, he thought, discernment and good sense in putting her finger on the source of the Church's troubles. The bishops *do* ordain men who have no title to any church and who fall into evil ways through idleness. Such men have no fear of punishment for they know the Church will defend them, and they know also that the bishops prefer crime to go unpunished rather than go to the trouble of doing their duty and putting these men in prison. Why, he wonders, is the Church so lax in dealing with obvious abuses?

'If you love the liberty of the Church,' he told Becket, 'for God's sake make it plain by word and deed that you are against these things. And if you write to the Empress, tell her so.'

On this evidence, Matilda seems to have had rather the better of the encounter with Becket's representative; but no effort she could make in the interests of peace was likely to have any success, for Becket was now taking his stand on the extreme view that the Church was supreme in the material, as well as in the spiritual sphere, and no king, least of all Henry, was likely to accept that.

By 1166, after two years of battle and abortive attempts at reconciliation, Becket prepared to take direct action against Henry. He wrote him three letters, in the last of which he warned him that if he did not pay heed to his warnings, he would 'experience the harshness of the divine vengeance'. To make sure that his warnings would have the maximum effect, he also wrote to a friend asking him to give a message to the Empress Matilda. His patience, he said, was exhausted. So 'let the Lady Empress know that in a short time – yea, in a very short time indeed – we shall, with God's help, unsheathe the sword of spirit, which is sharper than any two-edged sword, for the destruction of her son's sin-hardened flesh and the salvation of his soul which is sleeping – yea, asleep and near to death . . .'

Becket had a plan. He intended to go to the famous pilgrim church at Vézelay and there excommunicate Henry along with a number of other men whom he considered to be his enemies. In the event, he did not excommunicate Henry, for he had heard that the King was ill, perhaps dying, but he did excommunicate the others, flinging the lighted torches to the ground as he pronounced the sentences of damnation.

The whole thing fell rather flat, however, for the victims ignored the sentences for the most part, saying they had been given no warning nor any opportunity of defending themselves. As for Matilda, she was not at all impressed; in fact she is said to have treated the whole affair as something of a joke. 'What is the point of excommunicating such men?' she asked. 'Half of them were excommunicate already.' Clearly she, too, had lost patience.

The Pope himself now asked Matilda to make some effort at conciliation 'for the remission of her sins', and she did, in fact, write to Becket, though whether her letter was at all what the Pope had intended is quite another matter. She took Becket to task for showing gross ingratitude to the King for all the favours he had showered on him. His return for these favours had been to throw the whole realm into tumult and attempt his ruin. She wanted to know what his intentions were in relation to her son. His only hope of regaining the King's favour, she said, was by humbling himself and showing clear evidence of moderation. Perhaps he would let her know what he was prepared to do. Not unexpectedly, Becket seems to have made no reply to this. Humility and moderation were the very last things he appeared to have in mind at the moment.

Matilda did not live to see the end of the dispute, for she was now in the last year of her life. She was sixty-five, but still active and interesting herself closely in Henry's affairs.

He was once more at war with Louis of France, as he had been intermittently ever since he had married Eleanor fifteen years before; they had recently held an open-air conference at Gisors and they had parted in anger. Louis resented the loss of border fortresses in the Vexin, and they had also quarrelled furiously

over some money they had collected for the Holy Land. Both
demanded that it should be delivered by their own messengers;
and soon they were busy ravaging each other's lands.

It may have been during this campaign that Matilda organised
a spy service for Henry. She had become friendly with the Prior
of St Barbara near Lisieux, who was able to gather useful information about the movements of the enemy, and Matilda kept in
touch with him by employing as go-between a monk with an
exceptionally bushy beard; so bushy, in fact, that he was able to
hide messages in it with no risk of detection.

Matilda also played a part in bringing about the truce which
ended the hostilities. She wrote to Louis pleading common sense,
duty and religion as reasons for coming to a settlement, and the
terms agreed were those suggested by Matilda and the Count of
Flanders. Henry had destroyed Chaumont, so Louis was to be
allowed to destroy Les Andelys in return – after the inhabitants
had been evacuated.

It was almost her last public act, for she became seriously ill
soon afterwards, and prepared for death by taking the vows of a
nun of Fontévraud, although she still held by her wish to be
buried in the Abbey of Bec.

Henry was in Brittany when the news of his mother's illness
reached him, and he hurried to Rouen to be with her; but he was
too late. The Empress Matilda died on 9 September 1167. Her
other two sons had both died before her – Geoffrey in 1158 and
William in 1164 – but she had never seemed greatly interested in
them. It was Henry she loved.

Matilda's life falls into three distinct phases and she presents a
different picture in each of them; so different, in fact, that it is
difficult to fit them together into a coherent whole. There is the
'good Matilda' of her years in Germany, the 'arrogant' Matilda of
England, and the sage counsellor, the wise and pious old woman,
of her last years in Normandy. Historians, on the whole, have been
unfair to her in concentrating almost entirely on the unattractive
account of her given by English chroniclers at her moment
of triumph. But does this picture of Matilda as an arrogant,

bad-tempered, impossible woman stand up if opinions are put on one side and only facts considered? Not, it seems, during her years as Empress, for it is a fact that a number of nobles followed her when she left Germany and repeatedly begged Henry to allow her to stay with them. It is a fact that during the war with Stephen, she commanded the absolute loyalty of three remarkable men: Robert of Gloucester, Miles of Gloucester and Brian fitzCount. They were concerned, of course, to keep the oath they had sworn to uphold her claim to the throne; yet they had all broken this oath before she landed in England and had recognised Stephen as King. It is not very likely that regard for an oath, already broken, would alone have made them sacrifice so much, over so many years, if they had not been personally attached to Matilda as well.

It is also a fact that Henry II, a man of judgement and intelligence, valued her advice and sought it when he could; and on her side, she voluntarily relinquished her claim to the throne in his favour, not the action of an overweeningly arrogant woman. Lord Lyttelton, in fact, wrote of her in his biography of Henry II: 'There is not in all history another example of a woman who had possessed such high dignities and encountered such perils for the sake of maintaining her power, being afterwards content to give it up and, without forsaking the world, to live quietly in it.'

Yet whatever is said of Matilda, the central mystery remains. Why, at the most vital period of her life, did she behave with such arrogance and stupidity that she threw away all that she had fought for? There is no satisfying explanation. Perhaps the only certainty about Matilda is that she was brave; 'a woman girt about with fortitude', as the Archbishop of Rouen truly said of her.

Henry carried out his mother's wishes in giving large endowments to various religious establishments and charities in her name, and he also seems to have been responsible for the rather strange epitaph engraved on her tomb, which may be translated:

Here lies Henry's daughter, mother, wife.
Great in all three; her son the glory of her life.

It appears to be more in praise of himself than of her, and his own father Geoffrey receives no mention at all; but of course he was right. Matilda's greatest claim to immortality must rest on the fact that if she had not fought for her right to the English crown, and had not kept up the struggle until Henry was old enough to take it over, he might never have succeeded to the throne and England would have lost one of her greatest kings.

Bibliography✌✋

Anglo-Saxon Chronicle (Rolls Series), ed. B. Thorpe (London, 1861); translated by G. N. Garmonsway (revised ed., Everyman's Library, 1960)

Appleby, John T., *The Troubled Reign of King Stephen* (London, 1969)

Bagley, J. J., *Life in Mediaeval England* (London, 1960)

Bagley, J. J., Rowley, P. B., and Williams, E. N., *A Documentary History of England*, vol. 1 (London, 1966)

Barlow, F., *The Feudal Kingdom of England* (London, 1955)

Bouquet, Martin, *Recueil des Historiens de la France* (Paris, 1738–1904)

Brakelond, Jocelin of, *Chronicle*, ed. H. E. Butler (London, 1949)

Brooke, Christopher, *The Structure of Mediaeval Society* (London, 1971)

Brooke, Christopher, *The Saxon and Norman Kings* (London, 1963)

Bryce, J. V., *The Holy Roman Empire* (London, 1922)

Cambridge Mediaeval History, vol. v, ed. J. R. Turner (Cambridge, 1929–1932)

Canterbury, Gervase of, *Opera Historica* (Rolls Series), ed. W. Stubbs (London, 1879)

Coulton, G. G., *The Mediaeval Scene* (Cambridge, 1931)

Cronne, H. A., *The Reign of Stephen* (London, 1970)

Davis, H. W. C., *Henry of Blois and Brian Fitzcount*, English Historical *Review XXV* (London, 1910)

Davis, H. W. C., *England Under the Normans and Angevins* (London, 1905)

Davis, H. W. C., *Mediaeval Europe* (London, 1911)

Davis, R. H. C., *King Stephen* (London, 1967)

Delort, Robert, *Life in the Middle Ages* (London, 1974)

Douglas, David, *The Norman Fate* (London, 1976)

Durham, Simeon of, *Opera* (Rolls Series), ed. T. Arnold (London, 1882)

Fitznigel, Richard, *Dialogus de Scaccario*, ed. A. Hughes (London, 1902)

Freeman, E. A., *Reign of William Rufus* (Oxford, 1882)

Gesta Stephani Regis Anglorum, Anon. (Rolls Series), ed. Richard Howlett (London, 1886); ed. K. R. Potter (with translation) (London, 1955)

Green, J. R., *A Short History of the English People* (London, 1888)

Green, M. A. Everett, *Lives of the Princesses of England* (London, 1850)

Greenaway, George, *Life and Death of Thomas Becket* (London, 1961)

Hexham, Richard of, *De Gestis Regis Stephani* (Rolls Series), ed. R. Howlett (London, 1886)

Historia Gaufridi Ducis Normannorum (*Collections des textes pour l'étude de l'histoire*), ed. L. Halphen (Paris, 1913)

Huntingdon, Henry of, *Historia Anglorum* (Rolls Series), ed. T. Arnold (London, 1879)

Hutton, W. H., *St. Thomas of Canterbury* (London, 1899)

Kelly, Amy, *Eleanor of Aquitaine* (London, 1952)

Kelsey, Edward J., *Roger of Salisbury* (California, 1972)

Knowles, David, *The Episcopal Colleagues of Thomas Becket* (Cambridge, 1951)

Lees, Beatrice A., *The Central Period of the Middle Ages* (London, 1909)

Lisieux, Arnulf of, *Letters,* ed. F. Barlow

Malmesbury, William of, *Historia Novella* (Rolls Series), ed. W. Stubbs (London, 1887-9); ed. K. R. Potter (with translation) (London, 1955)

Malmesbury, William of, *De Gestis Regum* (Rolls Series), ed. W. Stubbs (London, 1887)

Map, Walter, *De Nugis Curialium*, ed. T. Wright (London, 1850)

Mommsen, T. E., and Morrison, K. F., *Imperial Lives and Letters of 11th Century* (Columbia, 1962)

Morey, A., and Brooke, C. N. L., *Letters and Charters of Gilbert Foliot* (Cambridge, 1967)

Morey, A., and Brooke, C. N. L., *Gilbert Foliot and His Letters* (Cambridge, 1965)

Mundy, John H., *Europe in the High Middle Ages* (London, 1973)

Newburgh, William of, *Historia Rerum Anglorum* (Rolls Series), ed. R. Howlett (London, 1884)

Norgate, Kate, *England Under the Angevin Kings* (London, 1887)

Onslow, Earl of, *The Empress Maud* (London, 1939)

Orderic Vitalis, *Historia Ecclesiastica*, ed. A. L. Prevost and L. Delisle (Paris, 1838-55)

Pernoud, Régine, *Eleanor of Aquitaine* (London, 1967)

Poole, A. L., *From Domesday Book to Magna Carta* (Oxford, 1951)

Power, Eileen, *Mediaeval English Nunneries* (Cambridge, 1922)

Quennell, C. H. B. and M., *A History of Everyday Things in England* (London, 1918)

Ramsay, Sir James, *The Angevin Empire* (Oxford, 1903)

Rievaulx, Aelred of, *Relatio de Standardo* (Rolls Series), ed. R. Howlett (London, 1886)

Robertson, J. C., and Sheppard, J. B., *Materials for the History of Thomas Becket* (London, 1875–85)

Rössler, Oskar, *Die Kaiserin Mathilde* (Berlin, 1897)

Round, J. H., *Geoffrey de Mandeville* (London, 1892)

Salisbury, John of, *Historia Pontificalis*, ed. Marjorie Chibnall (London, 1956)

Saltman, A., *Theobald, Archbishop of Canterbury* (London, 1956)

Slocombe, George, *The Sons of the Conqueror* (London, 1960)

Stenton, D. M., *English Society in the Early Middle Ages* (London, 1951)

Stenton, F. M., *The First Century of English Feudalism* (Oxford, 1932)

Stenton, F. M., *Norman London* (London, 1934)

Strickland, A., *Queens of England*, vol. 1 (London, 1840)

Stubbs, William, *The Early Plantagenets* (London, 1876)

Stubbs, William, *The Constitutional History of England* (London, 1891)

Tomkieff, O. G., *Life in Norman England* (London, 1966)

Torigni, Robert of, *Chronica* (Rolls Series), ed. R. Howlett (London, 1889)

Tout, T. F., *The Empire and the Papacy* (London, 1921)

Waddell, Helen, *Mediaeval Latin Lyrics* (London, 1929)

Warren, W. L., *Henry II* (London, 1973)

Wendover, Roger of, *Flores Historiarum*, ed. H. O. Coxe (London, 1841–4)

Worcester, Florence of, *Chronicon ex Chronicis & Continuation*, ed. B. Thorpe (London, 1848)

Index